Needlepoint
From
Start to Finish

The Complete Guide for Right and Left Handed Stitchers

Kim Cool

Iona Dettelbach

Computer Diagrams by Heidi Adams Coventry Cool

Fredericktown Press
Frederick, Maryland

©1992 Fredericktown Press
Second Printing 1993
ISBN: 09631976-0-6

Authors: Kim Cool and Iona Dettelbach

Printed in the United States of America by
Reproductions, Incorporated, Gaithersburg, Maryland

Dedication

We dedicate this book to Ron and Barbara Seres who recognized the need for a complete book on needlepoint for contemporary stitchers, to our graphic artist and editor, Heidi Cool, to the memory of Ken Cool who always believed we could if only we would and to Richard Dettelbach who offered great support and encouragement throughout the writing, to Martha Keane and Suzanne Powell who proofread the chapters on stitching and finishing. Most of all we would like to thank our parents Eva Patmore and the late Herman C. Patmore and Bea Schaffer and the late Louis L. Schaffer who taught us there was nothing we could not do nor learn, if we would only try.

Kim Cool and Iona Dettelbach
Cleveland, Ohio
December 1991

A Note To Stitchers

For well over 30 years we have been using our needles to combine fabrics and fibers and for all those years we have been grateful to the manufacturers who have continued to offer us new and improved materials and additional colors. When we mention a manufacturer in this book, it is because we truly believe in that company. You spend so much time in the creation of your needlework that your time alone merits your use of the finest materials. You should also consider the pleasure derived from working with finer materials - the feel of silk against fine cotton or linen canvas, for example.

Much of the joy we have received from our needlework is due in no small way to manufacturers such as Zweigart® who have always maintained the highest quality in the manufacture of needlepoint canvas. They have also been quick to respond to the consumer with additional colors and canvas mesh sizes. We believe so strongly in this company that we sell only Zweigart® needlepoint canvas in our retail store.

We would also like to acknowledge the contribution of Kreinik Manufacturing Company Inc. as one of the leaders in the development and distribution of imaginative fibers for the needleworker. Kreinik metallic threads include: Balger®, Japan Threads, Ombres, and Facets™. Kreinik also offers a wide variety of silk yarns and precious metal threads.

All of these fibers introduced by Kreinik makes stitching exciting and novel. We recommend them to our customers and use them in many of our own projects.

As you read through the pages of this book, you will learn about all the fibers and fabrics that we have experienced. We will share our preferences with you as well as the reasons for our preferences.

Table of Contents

Chapter 1 - Facts, Fabrics and Fibers..1

    Needlepoint Canvas..2
    Notions and Accessories..4
    Threads and Fibers..6
    Embellishments 9

Chapter 2 - Before the First Stitch 10

    Reading the Stitch Charts 11
    Mounting the Project on a Frame 11
    Threading the Needle..13
    Yarn Thickness..14
    Compensating Stitches..14
    Mistakes..14
    Left-handed Instructions..15
    Working Conditions..15

Chapter 3 - Stitches..16

    Tent Stitches..17
    Basketweave Directions for Right-handed Stitchers............................21
    Basketweave Directions for Left-handed Stitchers..............................25
    Straight Stitches..33
    Diagonal Stitches 43
    Cross Stitches..54
    Ties Stitches..75
    Decorative Stitches..84
    Alphabets..97

Chapter 4 - The Sampler Projects..99

    Pansy Centered Sampler..100
    Diagonal Striped Sampler..103
    Horizontal Striped Sampler for Advanced Stitchers............................107
    Bargello Band for Double Bow Pillow..112

Chapter 5 - Projects From Start to Finish..113

    Designing Your Project..113
    Oversized Projects..114
    Cleaning..116
    Blocking..117
    Hand Finishing..118
    Trims and Tassels..119
    Projects 121
    Machine Finishing..131
    Framing..136
    Preservation..136

Conclusion..137

CHAPTER ONE

FACTS, FABRICS AND FIBERS

Needlepoint or canvas embroidery is a stitchery technique used to create a durable fabric. Traditional embroidery and cross stitch are primarily fabric embellishment techniques. Needlepoint stitches wrap around the thread of the basic scrim or needlepoint canvas in such a way as to increase the strength of the canvas. This is why needlepoint has traditionally been the choice method for fine hand made rugs, purses and upholstery.

In ancient times when men fought for a living, women were the weavers and embroiderers. In the days before central heating, needlepoint was done for necessity as well as for pleasure. Large wall hangings and rugs served to keep dwellings warm. By the late middle ages, men left the battlefields for the fields of commerce. Exclusive guilds were formed by the men. Although they were excluded from the embroiderers guild, women were still allowed to do the weaving and the laborious hand-sewing. Court ladies and cloistered ladies continued to do decorative embroidery. In Spain, black work became a highly developed art. Nuns used white work and assisi embroidery for priestly vestments and ceremonial linens. While the new world was being developed, men were too busy clearing the land, plowing and planting, to worry about household items and clothing. It was here in America that women once again took up the needle for more than utilitarian items. All educated young women learned their letters and numbers as they learned their stitching on samplers, since women were expected to know how to mark their household linens. By the time of Queen Victoria, needlework had evolved to a very fine art and stitchers were fashioning all sorts of decorative items for their dress and for their homes. Just when needlework reached its zenith, the Industrial Age dawned. Everyone became fascinated by machines and things hand-made were called "home-made."

Today, "home-made" again means "hand-made" and such things are prized in our modern plastic world. Needlepoint is not "throw-away art". Go to any museum to see old pieces such as rugs, purses, samplers, and chairs which are highly prized and form the heart of many collections. Some of us are fortunate to have needlepoint chairs or rugs made by parents or grandparents. What you stitch today will be in your family for generations.

Needlepoint From Start to Finish features three sampler projects, one bargello pillow band, color pictures of needlepoint projects, and instructions for planning and finishing these items. Because needlepoint today is truly an art, these projects feature different fibers and stitches. All the painted canvases shown in the book are commercially available at your local needlework shop. While the designs are all pleasing it is the choice of fibers and stitches that has made them each so unique. We will tell you about fibers and canvas and we will show you seventy-one good basic stitches within the pages of this book. Keep this book in your needlework bag. Use different fibers and different sizes of canvas. Work from painted canvases or work from charts but make your needlepoint project your very own.

NEEDLEPOINT CANVAS

There are three types of needlepoint canvas - penelope, mono and interlock. The traditional canvas is a double thread canvas called Penelope and is usually a light tan color. As it is woven adjacent pairs of threads are squeezed together. Stitches covering the pairs of threads are called gros point. Stitches over the single threads are considered *petit point*. This canvas is particularly popular in Europe where both *gros point* and *petit point* are worked on the same canvas. Another feature of this double weave is the fact that you can do the half cross stitch when working over the pairs of threads. This stitch uses half as much yarn as most others. This is not a strong stitch because of its lack of backing and is best used only for pictures. Penelope canvas comes in various sizes such as 10/20, 12/24 and 18/36. The first number refers to the *gros point* stitches per inch and the second number refers to the *petit point* stitches per inch.

Mono canvas is a single thread canvas as the name implies. The threads of mono canvas are woven over one another, exactly as the pot holders you wove as a child. In Europe, mono is called "American canvas" as virtually all of it is exported to the United States. Mono canvas is available in many counts. The most popular sizes are 10,12,13,14 and 18, although 7, 16 and 17 and 24 are also available in some shops.

There is quite a broad spectrum of prices for this canvas. We have seen mono canvas priced as low as $8.00 per yard and as high as $28.00 per yard. If your inclination is to buy the cheaper canvas, please consider this fact. The average needlepoint project uses 1/4 yard of canvas. If you do some simple division, you will see that the cheaper canvas costs $2.00 for a piece this size and the most expensive canvas costs $7.00. A little subtraction will show you that there is only a $5.00 difference in the cost of your project . Since your project may take you several weeks or even months to complete and may use $15.00 or $30.00 worth of materials, it seems foolish to even consider the cheaper canvas.

If you are not yet convinced that "you get what you pay for," there is a simple test to determine the strength of the canvas and therefore the final strength of your finished needlepoint. Unravel one thread of the canvas and untwist that thread. The cheaper canvas will usually contain two skinny little threads and lots of sticky powdery stuff called sizing. That sizing will begin to vanish as you stitch and totally disappear when the canvas is wet for blocking. Do the same to a thread raveled from a piece of Zweigart® mono canvas. The better canvas will reveal up to six threads twisted together with very little sizing. This is obviously the stronger canvas.

Mono canvas is usually white although the 24 mesh also comes in yellow and peach. There is a tan mono canvas available in sizes 13 and 18. It is known as Bargello canvas and will feel rougher to the touch. This roughness helps to support the longer straight stitches used in Bargello or Florentine embroidery. We included a bargello pillow band in this book as an introduction to this colorful form of needlepoint.

Another type of mono canvas is called Congress cloth and is generally sold to cross stitchers. It is actually an 18 count needlepoint canvas. It comes in several colors which enable you to stitch a pleasing design without stitching the background.

The third canvas type is known as Interlock. It appears to be woven from a single thread. Actually woven from two threads which are interlocked around the warp thread as the canvas is loomed. It gains its strength from this interlock weave rather than from the thickness of the threads. Therefore it is not as strong as comparable mono canvas. It is the canvas of choice for items such as vests and tea cozies that require odd shapes to be cut from the canvas. Most pre-finished items such as eyeglass cases and tennis racket covers are made of interlock canvas. The fact that it does not stretch and drape well makes it ideal for the items just mentioned but makes it unsuitable for such items as rugs and upholstery. The locked threads also make this type of canvas unsuitable for certain stitching techniques such as pulled thread and drawn canvas work. We will be teaching you to do the Basketweave Stitch "on the grain." This technique is impossible on interlock canvas since the weave is not obvious.

All of the canvas discussed above is made of cotton. Most canvas is 40 inches wide although it is available in 54 inch width. Linen canvas is available and is very strong. Because linen is a vegetable fiber it is very soft and it stretches. Work linen canvas on a frame. For clothing items, a polyester garment canvas is available from Kreinik Mfg. which drapes beautifully. It is a #18 white mono interlock weave.

For true petit point which is finer than 18 mesh, silk gauze is available in such sizes as 24, 30, 40, and 56 threads per inch. These even count mono canvases are made with raw silk filaments, constructed in such a manner to insure the yarns will not slip while being stitched. Silk gauze is very costly and usually sold by the square inch.

If you come across something called "Waste Canvas," do not use it for needlepoint. It is made for putting cross stitch designs on fabric and is designed to practically self-destruct after stitching. Needless to say it would not be a good base for your needlepoint stitching. You will recognize it by its Penelope weave and the blue thread that is used for every tenth warp thread.

The warp thread is the vertical thread of the canvas. The horizontal threads are called the weft. To stitch on the straight grain you must keep the selvage edge to the right or left as you stitch. If the selvage has been cut from your canvas, unravel a thread from each side of a corner. The one that is slightly more ridged will be the warp thread and should run from top to bottom of your canvas. It is more ridged from the pressure put against it by the loom as the weft is inserted.

NOTIONS AND ACCESSORIES

You will need dress-making scissors for cutting your canvas and fine pointed embroidery scissors for clipping threads and removing incorrect stitches. <u>Never</u> use a seam ripper for anything to do with needlepoint! The fine pointed scissors will enable you to slip under the stitching thread and clip it without cutting your canvas. *(If you ever do cut your canvas, do not panic - simply weave in a new thread to replace the cut thread and stitch as though it never happened.)* Needlepointers use blunt-pointed tapestry type needles that come numbered as in the table below. Notice that the higher number signifies a smaller needle just as a higher number denotes a finer mesh canvas.

Size 13 needle 5 to the inch canvas
Size 16 needle 7 to the inch canvas
Size 18 needle 10 to the inch canvas
Size 20 needle 12 to the inch canvas
Size 22 needle 13 or 14 to the inch canvas
Size 24 needle 16, 17 or 18 to the inch canvas
Size 26 needle 24 to the inch canvas or silk gauze

To keep your needles clean and thus keep your work clean, a strawberry emery would be a nice addition to your work bag. Emery is a material used to polish metal. If you own a tomato pin cushion with a strawberry attached to it, the strawberry most likely is filled with emery. A needle threader is not a luxury item but a necessity for many stitchers. Sew it to the corner of your canvas so you will always have it handy. However, here is a hint for threading those tiny little needles. Take your thread and fold it over the needle and pull it very tight. Pinch this end very tightly between the thumb and forefinger of your left hand if you are right-handed and then

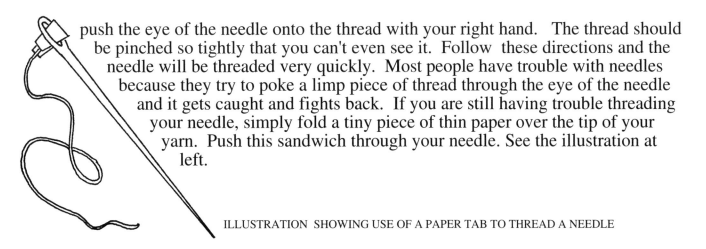

push the eye of the needle onto the thread with your right hand. The thread should be pinched so tightly that you can't even see it. Follow these directions and the needle will be threaded very quickly. Most people have trouble with needles because they try to poke a limp piece of thread through the eye of the needle and it gets caught and fights back. If you are still having trouble threading your needle, simply fold a tiny piece of thin paper over the tip of your yarn. Push this sandwich through your needle. See the illustration at left.

ILLUSTRATION SHOWING USE OF A PAPER TAB TO THREAD A NEEDLE

If you are used to a thimble, continue to use one. For smoothing your threads as you stitch, it is nice to have a bodkin or a "Trolley Needle™". Another nicety is a wonderful tote bag to hold all your work. It should have pockets for your scissors and stitch book and perhaps some loops for your threads. You should have a scissors case to protect your scissors. Loose scissors in a work bag could too easily damage both tote bag and needlework.

Needlepoint should never be done on an embroidery hoop. The hoop will crush the stitches. Experienced stitchers do all their work on rolling frames which come in many sizes. While a few stitchers are able to do very fine work without a frame, we feel that the best stitchers always use a frame. A frame forces one to take two steps with each stitch, poking the needle up from underneath the canvas and then back down to complete the stitch. The stitcher develops a rhythm that is constant and leads to a better finished project. If you decide that you enjoy needlepoint and want to do much more, we encourage you to try a frame. Give yourself a week; by then you should see the improvement in your stitching. **A note for left-handers:** needlework mounted on a frame frees left-handed stitchers from the laborious task of transposing numbers and changing all the rights to lefts in our instructions. Just make sure your left hand is on the bottom and your right hand on the top.

Whether you stitch on a frame or not, you will have to bind the rough edges of your canvas to protect your arms and your threads. You can sew seam binding on the edge of the canvas if you have a machine but inexpensive masking tape folded over the edge works just as well.

If you need to mark your canvas, be sure to use a water proof pen made for use on needlepoint canvases. Sanford makes the Nepo™ pen for this purpose. It comes in in several colors. Black is a good basic choice. If you make a mark and want to erase it, use white acrylic paint. Most any brand will do. If you want to color your canvas, use acrylic paint. Because of the new ecology laws, not all colors are color-fast so be sure to check each color you use by allowing it to dry on a scrap of needlepoint canvas and then wetting it to see if it bleeds or runs. This applies to paints as well as pens.

Tracing paper, newsprint and graph paper are all useful items to have for designing your own projects. Your local copy center will be helpful should you need to enlarge or shrink a design. Tracing paper is also useful for copying the outline of your project before you begin to stitch. Put the outline in a safe place until it is time to block your piece. You will want the blocked piece to match this original outline. This is especially important if you are making an odd-shaped project such as a three-dimensional animal.

THREADS AND FIBERS

Needlepoint in the past was done with natural fibers . Today there are also many wonderful synthetic fibers and blends, as well as metallics, ribbons and cords. Do not use the 4-ply knitting worsted known as sport yarn because it stretches and the fibers are too short, making it too weak for needlepoint. There are several knitting yarns that you can use. To test them, take a one yard piece and stitch with it. If it does not become quickly frayed, nor pilled, use it! You will usually be using the more readily available needlepoint materials such as tapestry, persian or crewel wool. While you are testing yarns, experiment with the plies needed for the stitches and canvas used in your project.

TAPESTRY WOOL is a four-ply wool that is not easily separated and thus should only be used on the 12, 13 or 14 to the inch canvas for which it is made. As the name implies, the colors are soft and muted as in aged tapestries. The color range is quite large.

MEDICI™ is a DMC brand name for a fine French wool embroidery yarn. You will use two or three ply on 18 to the inch canvas and one ply on 24 to the inch canvas.

PERSIAN WOOL comes in a brighter color range than other yarns. It was developed for use in Persian carpets and is a three plied yarn which is easily separated, fitting easily on most sizes of canvas. You will use three ply on 10 to the inch canvas, two ply on 12, 13 or 14 to the inch and one ply on 18 to the inch canvas. In our stitch directions you will note that some stitches will require more or less plies on the same mesh.

CREWEL WOOL is a finer thread usually dyed in colors similar to the tapestry yarns. Because it is very fine it can be plied many ways to fit anything from a size 10 to the inch canvas to the very fine 24 to the inch mesh. Many stitchers combine plies of different shades and actually "paint" the canvas with this yarn.
EMBROIDERY FLOSS is a shiny six ply cotton thread that is very versatile for needlepoint. Floss must be stripped or separated, no matter how many plies are to be used. This allows the threads to "bloom" or spread evenly over the canvas threads. Use at least nine ply on 13 mesh and five ply on 18 mesh. THE LEFT-

HANDED AUTHOR USUALLY USES ONE LESS PLY THAN THE RIGHT-HANDED AUTHOR. We don't know if this is a universal phenomenon but it does point out the need to experiment. All brands are not fully color-fast.

MATTE COTTON is a non-divisible soft matte finish thread available in a large range of tapestry colors. It will fit on 12, 13, or 14 to the inch canvas. It is not mercerized and is softer than embroidery floss. The words *Retor a Broider* are found on the label. You will have to use shorter strands. Matte cotton comes in a pull skein.

PERLE COTTON is a highly mercerized twisted non-divisible lustrous cotton thread. Size 3 will fit a 12, 13 or 14 to the inch canvas. Size 5 will fit an 18 to the inch canvas. Size 8 will fit a 24 inch mesh. To cut the skeins without removing the label, proceed as follows. Look for the end with two loops. Cut through all the threads at this end. You will also find a knot at this end. Cut it and remove it. To use one strand, go to the other end of your skein. Use a needle to lift one thread at a time. Pull out carefully, leaving the other threads in place with the label.

LINEN THREAD comes in a fairly short color range and you must buy enough yarn for your project because dye lots are very erratic. Linen comes in several sizes from very thick for 10 mesh canvas to very fine for 24 to the inch canvas. Linen is a vegetable fiber. There will be slight variations in thickness and color within the same skein. This is part of its charm. As it "blooms" or spreads over the canvas threads, the natural oil within the fibers is released. Because the linen will stay right where you place it, use a slightly looser tension than you would with other materials. It is difficult to remove linen stitches. Use size 10/5 on 10 mesh canvas, 10/2 on 13 mesh and 20/2 on 24 mesh canvas.

SILK THREAD is an animal fiber that is the lustrous product of the silk worm moth. When Japan went to war with the United States in World War Two, silk vanished almost overnight. Chemical companies created nylons and rayons and other synthetic fibers to fill the void. For most of the years since then, silk has been considered rare, expensive and delicate. The recent interest in natural fibers has spurred renewed interest in silk.

Silk comes in many types. Silk such as Au ver a Soie from Kreinik Mfg. Co. Inc. has a soft sheen. It is easier to use than cotton because it is "smooth" while cotton is "fuzzy." Silk is stronger than cotton, has a translucency that absorbs and reflects light, and has three times more yardage per opound than cotton of equal diameter. Because of its smooth surface, silk flows easily through needlework fabrics. The color range is vast but here again, the dye lots are very different so you must buy enough material for a project. Kreinik Mfg. Co. Inc. offers the following types of silk: Soie d'Alger, Soie Gobelins, Soie Perlee, Soie Platte, Soie Noppee, and Ping Ling. We recommend that silk should be dry-blocked and dry-cleaned. If you are using multiple fibers, stitch those that can be wet-blocked first; after blocking, stitch your silk threads.

METAL THREADS (REAL) are available in different shapes and sizes such as

Passing Threads, Buillions, Friezes, Faconnes, Jacerons, and Cordonnets. Most are laid and couched in place for a dimensional unique texture.

METALLIC THREAD comes in many wonderful colors and different weights and textures. Kreinik Mfg. Co. Inc. developed metallics which include Blending Filaments, Cords, Cables, Fine (#8) Braid, Medium (#16) Braid, Heavy (#32) Braid, 1/16" Ribbon and 1/8" Ribbon. All of these are washable, dry-cleanable and easily stitchable. Metallics are actually polyester fibers and extremely easy to handle. Blending filaments were developed for cross stitch and can be blended with other fibers for needlepoint. Kreinik 1/8" Ribbon for 13 mesh canvas and 1/16" Ribbon for 16 or 18 mesh canvas. Kreinik Ombre is a soft 8-ply metallic thread, adaptable to any canvas mesh. Facets™ is a multi-dimensional, bead-like thread that is couched for exquisite outlining. All these threads create a life-like dimension and add a lovely source of "light" to all designs. Your shop will help you select the proper size and type of metallic threads for your canvas.

Chainette is a different type of metallic thread. It looks like a chain of crochet stitches and will unravel. Never cut chainette. Break it to lock the stitches. Our favorite chainette is Cloissone™ from Johnson's Creative Arts. It fits size 10 or 12 mesh canvas.

RAYON RIBBON is available in two weights. There are plain colors and metallics as well as over-dyed. Ribbonfloss™ fits am 18 mesh caanvas and Melrose Krystal™ ribbon fits 13 mesh. Raclette™ is a translucent ribbon tube which has another fiber drawn through it.

RAYON FLOSS AND CORD are very bright and shiny. Rayon fibers are very slippery and difficult to stitch. The flosses tend to kink and knot. The ends must be carefully worked into your backing as they have a strong tendency to pull loose. The Chinese call rayon synthetic silk. Like silk, it is so beautiful on your canvas that it is well worth the aggravation. Unlike silk, it is inexpensive. Some stitchers wet the threads before stitching as a way of controlling the fibers.

WATERCOLORS™ is the brand name of plied twisted cotton which appears variegated. Some skeins are blends of a single color while other skeins are combinations of contrasting colors. It comes three ply to a strand. Use as is on 12 mesh canvas and divide for 13, 14 or 18. Try using this fiber with some of the fancy stitches such as Waffle, Scotch, and Montenegrin.

WATERLILIES™ SILK is died like WATERCOLORS™ but the fiber is silk. It is a stranded fiber. Use as you would silk.

Other fibers you can use for special effects include Alpaca, Angora, Berber Wool, Patent Leather, Ultra Suede™, and Veloura™.

We know this list is not complete as each day brings new fibers to your local stores. Try them as you needlepoint.

8

Add an element of surprise to your canvas with embellishments. Make the dew drop on your rose a sparkling "sew on" rhinestone. In addition to beads and buttons, "sew on" rhinestones and charms have recently become available in needlepoint shops. They are marketed under the name Charming Glitters™ by Kappie Originals Ltd. Look at the models pictured in this book for other ideas. Hot glue an appropriate miniature to the frame of your next needlepoint picture. These miniatures are available at craft and miniature stores. Use a string of miniature twinkle **lights attached to a music button on your child's Christmas stocking.**

The best embellishments of all are the stitches. Some of the prettiest needlepoint we have ever seen has been white. It is the stitches and the play of light dancing across them that create the elegant design. You may never use a glitter or glitz or any fiber other than wool but if you learn the stitches of needlepoint you will always be able to create a unique work of art.

CHAPTER TWO

BEFORE THE FIRST STITCH

PREPARING THE THREADS

We suggest you work most materials in 16 inch lengths. No thread should be longer than 18 inches since needlepoint canvas is very abrasive. If you are working with soft novelty threads you may wish to cut the threads as short as 12 inches. Silk, linen and matte cotton should be cut no longer than 14 inches in order to preserve their finish.

Cutting the threads. Any threads put up as Pull Skeins such as **MATTE COTTON** can simply be pulled from the skein to the proper length and then cut. We find it convenient and time-saving to thread several needles at once. Threads put up in twisted skeins such as **MEDICI**™ and **PERLE COTTON** need to be cut. These skeins are twisted and then folded before labeling. You must not cut the folded end. Instead, look at the other end of the skein which has two loops. Cut all the way through both of these loops. One of them will have a knot which you must also cut and remove from your skein. Leave the labels in place and you now have a pull skein with all your threads cut to 16 inches, the best length for stitching with these fibers. If you are using **PERSIAN YARN** from a quarter pound hank, you will want the hank to be opened and cut once near the knot so that all the yarn is in 62 inch lengths. If you plan to use one or three plies you may then choose to cut these strands in thirds or fourths for the best stitching length. If you are working with two ply you should cut your strands once and then use one ply doubled. (*If you use this method, you can start your thread by stitching through the loop on the back of your canvas made by folding the thread in half.*) Note, when using this loop method, one half of your thread will be running against the grain of the other half of the thread. This will give you a fuller though fuzzier look. If you want all your threads to have matching grains, do not use this method. **SILK THREAD** such as Au Ver a Soie must be completely separated and untwisted from one another in order to take full advantage of the reflective quality of the silk. **MATTE COTTON** and similar soft fibers which are not mercerized will snag and fray if worked with threads longer than 12 to 14 inches. **LINEN THREAD**, a natural vegetable fiber, also tends to break down when the threads are too long. You will even see a change in color. **RAYON THREAD** and similar slippery synthetics must be carefully anchored at the beginnings and the end of each thread. We recommend that you weave your beginnings and endings in two directions like the letter "Z."

READING THE STITCH CHARTS

The charts for the individual stitches used in this book are numbered in the standard method. The needle comes **up** from behind the canvas on the **odd** number and plunges **down** into the canvas on the **even** number. Project charts are to be used for placement of stitches. Only the beginning stitches are shown in detail. You will find instructions for all the stitches used in any of the projects in the stitch chart section of the book. The large project charts will also tell you the number of threads covered horizontally and vertically and the number of threads individual groups of stitches occupy as well as noting the center of the canvas when necessary. Following the stitch charts will be graphs of useful alphabets. Each mark on the chart represents one tent stitch. Use these alphabets to personalilze your projects.

MOUNTING A PROJECT ON A FRAME

We recommend that you use either a standard needlepoint roller bar frame or simple stretcher bars of the proper size for your project. The use of a frame frees both of your hands for stitchery and goes along way towards keeping your canvas square. You will work on a frame with your dominant hand underneath and the other hand on top. As you poke your needle up and down with your hands in this position, you will develop a rhythm that will keep your stitches even and keep your threads from twisting. The stitches that use tension such as buttonhole and chain stitches must be worked on a frame. Stitches that require the canvas threads to be pulled tightly, such as eyelet stitches, _must_ be worked on a frame.
To mount your canvas on a roller bar frame: first mark the centers of your roller bars with a waterproof pen, next mark the centers of the top and bottom of your actual canvas. Matching the marks, sew the canvas to the tape of the roller bar. If the roller bar is slotted, slide the canvas through the slot, match the centers and

11

tape in place with masking tape. Insert the roller bars into the side bars and roll the canvas until taut. You may roll your work either way illustrated below. You will have more control of your stitches with the method shown to the left but will keep your work cleaner with method shown to the right. We personally prefer the first method but remind you that you must never begin stitching without first washing your hands carefully.

ILLUSTRATION ON LEFT SHOWS CANVAS ROLLED OVER TOP EDGES OF FRAME.

ILLUSTRATION ON RIGHT SHOWS CANVAS ROLLED WITH WORK ON INSIDE.
EITHER METHOD IS CORRECT.

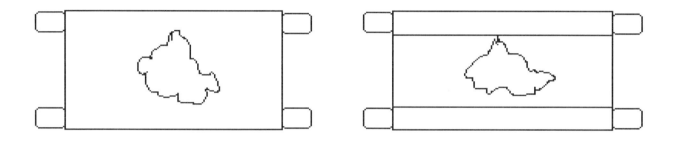

Newspapers should be kept away from your needlepoint. The print on your newspaper will be permanent on your needlework.

If you are using stretcher bars, they should be the size of the outer dimension of your canvas. You should use a staple gun with 1/4 inch staples to attach the canvas to the bars. The canvas should be stretched as tightly as possible. Make sure the canvas is not crooked.

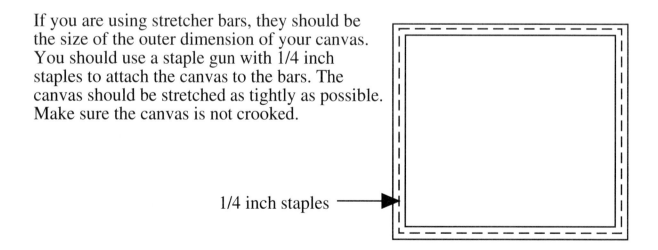

1/4 inch staples

ILLUSTRATION OF CANVAS MOUNTED ON STRETCHER BARS

Take your thread and fold it over the needle and pull it very tight. Pinch this end very tightly between the thumb and forefinger of your left hand if you are right-handed and then push the eye of the needle onto the thread with your right hand. The thread should be pinched so tightly that you can't even see it. Follow these directions and the needle will be threaded very quickly. Most people have trouble with needles because they try to poke a limp piece of thread through the eye of the needle and it gets caught and fights back. It is perfectly permisssible to use a needle threader but it should be one made for tapestry work. Your local store will probably have several choices for you. The third method involves cutting a smaller triangular from a piece of a slick paper magazine, as illustrated to the right.

When needlepointing, never knot the yarn. To take the first stitch, leave a tail of yarn about one inch long. As you follow the stitch chart, be sure to catch in the end of the tail as you stitch. Or use the loop method mentioned earllier if using two ply thread. A third method is to use a waste knot on the top of your canvas about one inch away from the beginning stitch but placed so you will stitch over the tail as you approach it. When the thread is covered the knot is cut off your canvas.

To end your thread, weave the tail in and out on the wrong side of the canvas, being sure you always weave vertically or horizontally, not at an angle. Clip the tail of your thread close to your work. Long tails tend to involve themselves in other stitches. If you are using a stitch that has little backing, it may be difficult to secure the tail of the thread. In this case, weave it over and under a few threads of canvas which will be covered by the next group of stitches.

Try not to start and stop in the same area. In working various areas of the same color, carry your thread no more than five or six stitches in any direction. Threads carried over long distances tend to creat lumps and bumps that do not block. Be especially careful of your stitching tension if you carry threads across your canvas. Whenever possible, weave these threads through existing stitches on the back of your canvas. Do not weave dark threads into light threads and vice versa.

Whenever possible, try not to sew into the back of existing stiches as you begin a new stitch. The charts in this book have been designed so that you generally will be working from open canvas into finished stitches.

13

Your tension should be as even and taut. Tight stitches will warp your canvas permanently while stitches that are too loose will be sloppy. Longer stitches require **slightly more tension than shorter stitches require.**

Various stitches require different thicknesses of yarn. The instructions with our stitch charts will suggest the number of strands of persian wool you need to stitch on a 13 to the inch canvas. <u>If you use other mesh sizes or different fibers, you will have to make adjustments.</u> A few stitches on the margin of your canvas will help you to quickly determine if you need to add or subtract strands for coverage of the canvas.

All ply materials should be separated, allowed to untwist and be put back together before they are stitched on a needlepoint canvas.

<u>Backing</u> refers to the amount of padding of fibers on the back of your needlepoint after stitching. This padding differs according to the stitch chosen. We will note the backing strength of each stitch in our charts so that you will be able to choose your stitches in proportion to the amount of wear your project must sustain.

<u>Compensating Stitches</u> are small stitches you will use to complete an area that is smaller than the whole decorative stitch you are working. The easiest method of fitting a decorative stitch into a design is to stitch a row across the widest part of the area. Work above and below this row with as much of each stitch as possible, compensating as necessary.

<u>Mistakes</u>. We all make mistakes and occasionally need to remove a stitch or two. If you catch your error while stitching, simply unthread your needle. pull out the incorrect stitch, rethread your needle and restitch. If you are dissatisfied with a stitch you worked a while back or don't care for the color in a certain area you will have to cut those stitches to remove them. To do this, carefully cut the wrong stitches with your embroidery scisssors on the right side of your canvas. Never use a seam ripper. It will probably cut the canvas. After you have cut the stitches to be removed, turn your work to the back side and pull out the work with a tweezers or with your needle. Little left-over wisps of thread can be removed with masking or cellophane tape. If you do cut your canvas, simply reweave a thread through the cut area , leaving a 2 inch tail at either end. After you have stitched over the repaired section, clip the tail ends close to the canvas. If you have torn several threads you will have to patch your canvas. To do this, cut a piece of canvas from the margin of your canvas, preferably on the same warp or weft and place it behind the torn section. Stitch through both layers of canvas and progress with your project.

LEFT-HANDED INSTRUCTIONS: Since one of the authors of this book is actually left-handed, all of our instructions will tell you left-handers how to turn the chart so that you may comfortably work the stitch. However, the left-handed author will remind you, if you work on a frame as she does, you will be able to comfortably follow most charts as they are presented.

Whether you are scoop-stitching or working on a frame you may feel more comfortable starting your needlework at the lower left hand corner of the large project charts.

Working Conditions. Try to do your stitching as far away as possible from snacks, pets, beverages, and newspapers. Lighted cigarettes will burn your work, ashes will soil it and the smoke will make it smell bad. If you smoke, or if you have otherwise **soiled your needlework it will be necessary to clean your project before finishing.** You will find how to instructions in the chapter on finishing.

CHAPTER THREE

STITCHES

The easiest way to learn needlepoint is to work a stitch sampler. There are three included in this book. Use these to learn your stitches or, better yet, create your own sampler on a blank piece of canvas. You will not be limited by design considerations and may practice a stitch until you are comfortable with it before going on to the next stitch. You can experiment with color combinations and scale of stitches. You can even leave stitches in various stages of completion. This sampler will be a valuable guide that you will use for years. In earlier days, samplers were passed from generation to generation. One of the most valuable embroideries in America is a family stitch sampler found in the Valentine Museum in Richmond, Virginia. It was stitched over many years by many generations. This sampler is so long that it is displayed by being folded back on itself as it wraps around the perimeter of its own room.

In this chapter you will find diagrams for seventy-one basic needlepoint stitches. The diagrams will be numbered to show the stitch sequence. Your needle will come up from behind the canvas on the odd number and plunge down into the canvas on the even number. The stitch sequences are designed for minimum canvas distortion and maximum stitch backing. Good backing increases the durabiltiy of the needlepoint project. Most stitches will require some compensation stitches. The compensation stitches will be shaded. The base stitches will be white. In addition to the diagrams, we will include notes to go with each stitch. The notes will pertain to the speed and wearability of each stitch. We will only note yarn usage for those stitches which are either yarn hogs are yarn savers. We suggest you stitch a test sample of each stitch you plan to use with the specific fibers you plan to use. Your requirements will change from project to project according to the canvas mesh size and the stitches and fibers chosen. Special instructions for left-handers will accompany each diagram.

Even though you believe your hands are clean, <u>wash them once again</u> before you begin to stitch. If you have been straightening magazines, petting the dog, rubbing your eyes, etc., you have been picking up minute particles of dirt which can permanently damage your work. The ink in today's newsprint trasfers easily to your hands and then to your needlepoint. Never keep newspapers near your work basket. If you are working on a frame, cover the frame when you quit working, to keep dust particles from settling on your work. If you smoke, do not smoke near your needlepoint, especially if you plan to give it to a non-smoking friend. Wool is porous and everything you stitch will smell as though you stitched it in "Marlboro™ Country."

Thread your needle with any old kind of yarn. Grab a piece of canvas and stitch along with us while you read the instructions and look at the stitch diagrams. Place the selvage edge to the left or right and mark the top of your canvas with a "safe" pen, described on page 5. Now, remove the selvage and bind all four raw edges with tape. The stitches you are about to learn will be with you always. As you combine them in various ways on your needlework you will become a needle artist. The satisfaction that you will have from creating your own needlepoint project is nothing compared to the joy of seeing it being used and admired.

We have divided the stitches in this book into six categories. The categories are designated as follows: Tent Stitches, Straight Stitches, Diagonal Stitches, Cross Stitches, Tied Stitches and Decorative Stitches.

TENT STITCHES

Tent Stitches are the oldest and most widely used stitches in canvas embroidery. When people think of needlepoint, these are the stitches they visualize. There are three Tent Stitches; Basketweave Stitch, Continental Stitch and Half-Cross Stitch.

A word about the Tent Stitch and Needlepoint Canvas. All Tent Stitches are diagonal stitches which run from lower left to upper right over an intersection of the canvas. A diagonal row of these stitches running from lower left to upper right will appear to be a solid straight line. A similar row, running from the lower right to the upper left will appear to be a dotted straight line, as illustrated to the right.

ILLUSTRATION SHOWING
SLANT OF TENT STITCH

This does not disturb most needlepointers because they understand that it is the nature of the art. However, some stitchers are extremely unhappy about this spotted look. If this is a problem you could do all your outlines in Chain Stitch which will emphasize the outline rather than blending it in with your stitching but you will obtain smooth edges to all your shapes. There are instructions for the Chain Stitch in this book on page 88. If you feel you must use this method, we feel it is best to do the outlining last, unlike the continental stitch outline which is done first. Be sure to leave the outline areas unstitched, in preparation for the Chain Stitch. Your outline will then fit nicely into your design and your other stitches will not become tangled with the Chain Stitch. You should use 1 ply less for your chain stitch than you have used for your Basketweave or other stitches.

Please resist the urge to turn your Tent Stitches in two directions. We much prefer the look of a Chain Stitch if you must have smooth edges.

BASKETWEAVE OR DIAGONAL TENT STITCH

Durable background or design stitch, little canvas distortion, **snagproof**, minimum texture and average stitching speed.

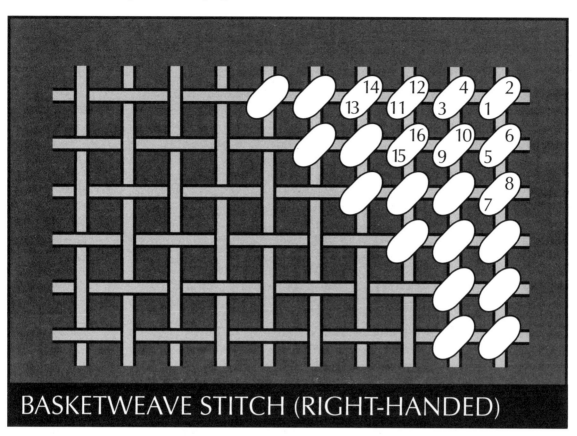

BASKETWEAVE STITCH (RIGHT-HANDED)

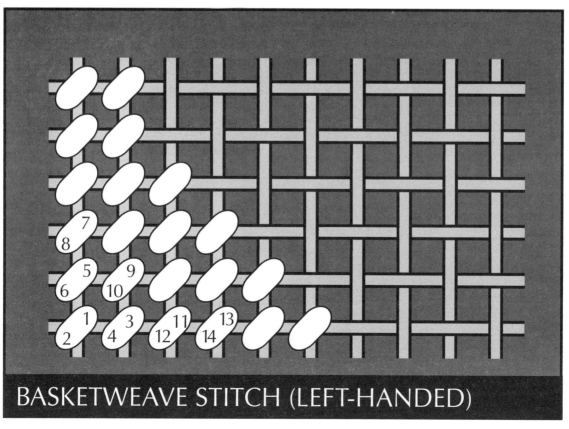

BASKETWEAVE STITCH (LEFT-HANDED)

Some stitchers go through their whole lives working all their needlepoint projects in the Continental Tent Stitch. These people are doing themselves and their needlework a diservice. In earlier days, stitchers were confined to penelope canvas which was often covered by trame threads. For this type canvas, continental or half cross were the stitches of choice. Today's stitchers buy designs that are brightly painted on modern mono-weave canvas. There is little justification for using the Continental Stitch. Basketweave Stitch or Diagonal Tent Stitch is rhythmic and relaxing. You will find that the backing, which looks like a woven basket, is strong and durable. This basketweave effect on the back is what keeps the canvas straight and true and gives the stitch its popular nickname. Once the stitch has been mastered and is worked in rhythm, the stitcher will notice how even their stitching looks, and how little the canvas has been distorted. In our own shop, we teach the basketweave stitch to new stitchers, reserving the Continental Stitch only for necessary outlining.

Complete Basketweave Stitch instructions will be found on the following pages. We are including explicit instructions and diagrams for both right and left-handed stitchers. Read whichever section pertains to you. Be sure to have a piece of canvas and a threaded needle handy so that you can stitch as you read.

BASKETWEAVE DIRECTIONS FOR RIGHT-HANDED STITCHERS

We will start you with a long diagonal row so that you can become comfortable with the basic si-titching method. At the end of this diagonal row is a stitch that is commonly referred to as the "turning stitch." It really is the first stitch of the new row. **Note: In the illustration the "turning stitch" is a shade lighter than the regular stitches.**

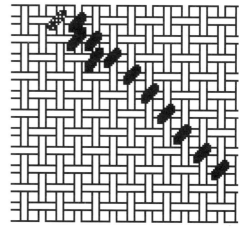

ILLUSTRATION SHOWS A COMPLETED
"UP" ROW OF BASKETWEAVE

The most common error when stitching Basketweave Stitch is to omit the "turning stitch" or to go to the other extreme and work it twice. If you have mistakes in your stitching pattern, check this area first.

Notice as you stitch this first diagonal row, that you are creating a saw-tooth pattern. The stitches of the next row will fit between the stitches of the first row just like the teeth of a zipper. If your stitches do not mesh in this manner, you have made an error. **STOP.** Unthread your needle and remove the incorrect stitches. It is always best to remove incorrrect stitches right away. The interweaving which makes the Basketweave Stitch so durable is also what makes the stitch so **difficult** to remove.

Another caution - Basketweave Stitch correctly done progresses up and down the canvas in <u>continuous diagonal rows.</u> Never work two up rows nor two down rows next to each other. Doing this causes an ugly ridge which is impossible to fix. There are two easy ways to avoid this mistake. Number one is to always end your work session either half way up or down a row with your needle in place for the next stitch. The second way is more basic and one that we will teach you - <u>read the grain of the canvas.</u>

21

Once you have learned to "read" your canvas, you will be able to work sections of Basketweave Stitch that are scattered. You will be secure in the knowledge that your basketweave pattern will mesh perfectly when all the scattered sections are joined. You will also understand why more experienced stitchers rarely use interlocked canvas which has no grain.

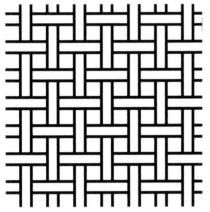

Take a piece of mono canvas. Notice that it is a simple over and under weave just like those pot-holders you wove as a child. Look at the illustration to the left.

The vertical threads are the warp threads of the canvas and the horizontal threads are the "weft " or "woof" threads.

ILLUSTRATION OF CANVAS WEAVE

Take a hard pencil or needlepoint marking pen and mark an intersection near the center of the canvas. If the intersection is topped by a verticaal thread, make a mark. If the intersection is topped by a horizontal thread, move the pencil right or left one intersection to a vertical and make a mark.

Now move your pen to the closest vertical intersection, below and to the right. Mark this intersection and continue doing so until you have marked at least ten intersections. This will mark the first row of your basketweave lesson. As you are right-handed, this diagonal row will proceed from upper left corner to lower right corner.

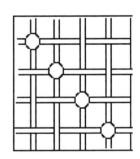

ILLUSTRATION SHOWING
MARKED VERTICAL INTERSECTIONS

It is time to start stitching!

Start at the upper left of the line you have just marked. As you work from stitch to stitch down the diagonal to the right, you will notice that the needle points in a vertical direction as it moves under two threads of the canvas to get to the next stitch.

When you have completed at least ten vertical stitches down the diagonal you will be at the lower right of your stitch sample. It is now time to work your first "turning" stitch. You will be covering the intersection immediately below the last intersection covered. To get there, insert your needle as if to do one additional vertical stitch, swing it one thread to the left so that your needle comes out below and to the left of the intersection to be covered. See illustration to the right. The point of the needle is in the circle at the bottom. The circled area is the "turning" stitch or the first stitch in the other direction.

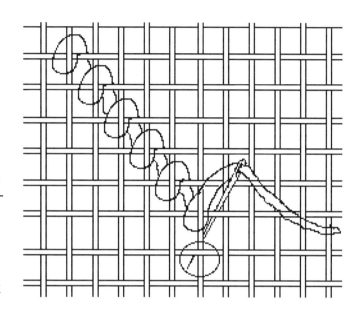

ILLUSTRATION OF TURNING STITCH

As you finish this "turning" stitch you will see that you have covered a horizontal intersection of your canvas. There is a whole row of these horizontal intersections forming a stairway back to the top of your stitch sample. To do the next stitch, insert your needle below and to the left of the next horizontal intersection to your left on the diagonal. Note that your needle is in a horizontal position and that you will be covering horizontal intersections. As you progress from one stitch to another your needle will again go under two threads of canvas. Continue in this manner, working up the horizontal intersections until you have reached the top of your stitch sample. Your last uphill stitch will be immediately to the left of the very first stitch you made when you began this sample piece.

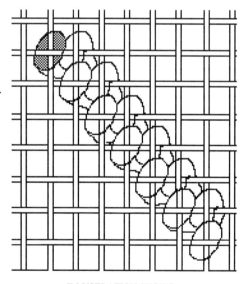

ILLUSTRATION SHOWS
LAST UPHILL STITCH AS SHADED AREA.

It is time for another "turning stitch." This stitch will be immediately to the left of the last uphill stitch and will cover a vertical intersection. Obviously, this vertical intersection signals the downhill row that you are about to begin. Continue back and forth for several diagonal rows until you feel confident that you are not forgetting your "turning stitches."

23

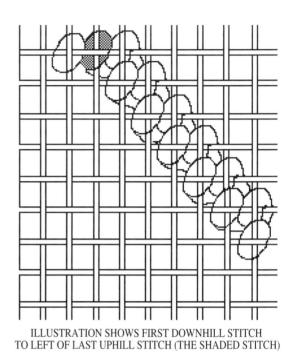

ILLUSTRATION SHOWS FIRST DOWNHILL STITCH
TO LEFT OF LAST UPHILL STITCH (THE SHADED STITCH)

The final test will be for you to convert this sample to a square as shown on the diagram below.

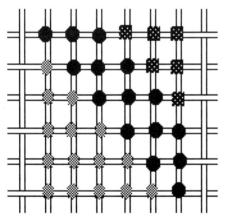

The black circles have been stitched and you must now stitch the light grey circles. After you have detached your thread, find the upper right corner area signified by the dark patterned squares and fill in those stitches. If you have successfully followed the grain of your canvas, your basketweave pattern will mesh perfectly as you join your stitch sections. As long as you follow the grain of the canvas in this manner you will always be able to use Basketweave Stitch, even when the area to be filled is not a square. In those areas, your turning stitch will simply be the closest intersection of the next diagonal row.

Now you are beginning to basketweave, a further hint. When starting and stopping new threads, do not run them on the diagonal. Instead, run them parallel to the vertical and horizontal threads of your canvas.

24

BASKETWEAVE DIRECTIONS FOR LEFT-HANDED STITCHERS

We will start you with a long diagonal row so that you can become comfortable with the basic stitching method. At the end of this diagonal row is a stitch that is **commonly** referred to as the "turning stitch." It really is the first stitch of the new row. **Note: In the illustration the "turning stitch" is a shade lighter than the regular stitches.**

ILLUSTRATION SHOWS A COMPLETED "UP" ROW OF BASKETWEAVE

The most common error when stitching Basketweave Stitch is to omit the "turning stitch" or to go to the other extreme and work it twice. If you have mistakes in your stitching pattern, check this area first.

Notice as you stitch this first diagonal row, that you are creating a saw-tooth pattern. The stitches of the next row will fit between the stitches of the first row just like the teeth of a zipper. If your stitches do not mesh in this manner, you have made an errror. **STOP.** Unthread your needle and remove the incorrect stitches. It is always best to remove incorrect stitches right away. The interweaving which makes the Basketweave Stitch so durable is also what makes the stitch so difficult to remove.

Another caution - Basketweave Stitch correctly done progresses up and down the canvas in continuous diagonal rows. Never work two up rows nor two down rows next to each other. To do so will cause an ugly ridge which is impossible to fix. There are two easy ways to avoid this mistake. Number one is to always end your work session either half way up or down a row with your needle in place for the next stitch. The second way is more basic and one that we will teach you - read the grain of the canvas.

Once you have learned to "read" your canvas, you will be able to work sections of Basketweave Stitch that are scattered. You will be secure in the knowledge that your basketweave pattern will mesh perfectly when all the scattered sections are joined. You will also understand why more experienced stitchers rarely use inter-locked canvas which has no grain.

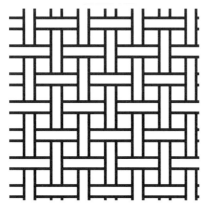

Take a piece of mono canvas. Notice that it is a simple over and under weave just like those pot-holders you wove in first grade. Look at the illustration to the left.

The vertical threads are the warp threads of the canvas and the horizontal threads are the "weft" or "woof" threads.

ILLUSTRATION OF CANVAS WEAVE

Take a hard pencil or needlepoint marking pen and mark an intersection near the center of the canvas. If the intersection is topped by a verticaal thread, make a mark. If the intersection is topped by a horizontal thread, move the pencil right or left one intersection to a vertical and make a mark.

Now move your pen to the nearest vertical intersection, above and to the left. Mark this intersection and continue doing so until you have marked at least 10 intersections. This will mark the first row of your basketweave lesson. Because you are left-handed this diagonal row will proceed from lower right corner to upper left corner.

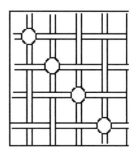

ILLUSTRATION SHOWING
MARKED VERTICAL INTERSECTIONS

It is time to start stitching!

Start at the lower right of the line you have just marked. As you work from stitch to stitch up the diagonal to the left, you will notice that the needle points in a vertical direction as it moves under 2 theads of the canvas to get to the next stitch, as illustrated.

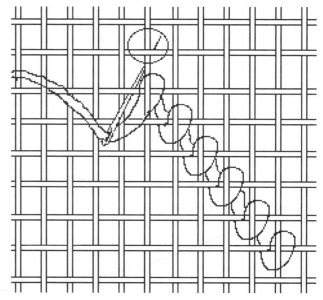

ILLUSTRATION OF TURNING STITCH

When you have completed at least ten vertical stitches up the diagonal you will be at the upper left of your stitch sample. It is time to work your first "turning" stitch. You will be covering the intersection immediately above the last intersection covered. To get there, insert your needle as if to do one additional vertical stitch, swing it one thread to the right so that your needle comes out above and to the right of the intersection to be covered. See illustration above. The point of the needle is in the circle at the top of the illustration.

The circled area is the "turning" stitch or the first stitch in the other direction.

As you finish this "turning" stitch you will see that you have covered a horizontal intersection of your canvas. There is a whole row of these horizontal intersections forming a stairway back to the bottom of your stitch sample. To do the next stitch, insert your needle above and to the right of the next horizontal intersection on the diagonal. Note that your needle is in a horizontal position and that you will be covering horizontal intersections. As you progress from one stitch to another your needle will again go under two threads of canvas. Continue in this manner, working down the horizontal intersections until you have reached the bottom right of your stitch sample. Your last downhill stitch will be immediately above the very first stitch you made when you began this sample piece.

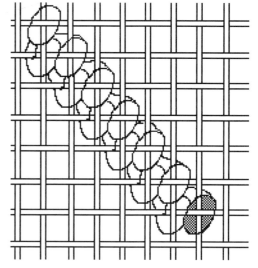

ILLUSTRATION SHOWS LAST DOWNHILL STITCH AS SHADED AREA.

27

It is time for another "turning stitch." This stitch will be immediately to the right of the last downhill stitch and will cover a vertical intersection. Obviously, this vertical intersection signals the uphill row that you are about to begin. Continue back and forth for several rows until you feel confident that you are not forgetting your "turning" stitches.

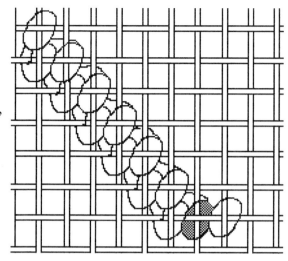

ILLUSTRATION SHOWS FIRST UPHILL STITCH
TO RIGHT OF LAST DOWNHILL STITCH (THE SHADED STITCH)

The final test will be for you to convert this sample to a square
as shown on the diagram below.

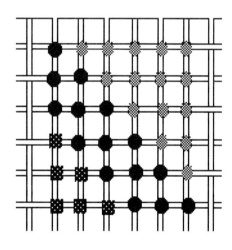

The black circles have been stitched and you must now stitch the light grey circles. After you have detached your thread, find the lower left corner area signified by the dark patterned squares and fill in those stitches. If you have successfully followed the grain of your canvas, your basketweave pattern will mesh perfectly as you join your stitch sections. As long as you follow the grain of the canvas in this manner you will always be able to use Basketweave Stitch, even when the area to be filled is not a square. In those areas, your turning stitch will simply be the closest intersection of the next diagonal row.

Now you are beginning to basketweave, a further hint. When starting and stopping new threads, do not run them on the diagonal. Instead, run them parallel to the vertical and horizontal threads of your canvas.

28

CONTINENTAL STITCH

Continental Stitch provides good backing, is snag-proof, has minimum texture, and is fairly quick to stitch but causes extreme canvas distortion. This variation of the tent stitch uses the same amount of yarn as basketweave.

Continental Stitch differs from Basketweave Stitch in that adjacent stitches are worked in any direction along a stright line, vertically, horizontally, or diagonally. It is the stitch's versatility in this regard that makes it the top choice for outlining. It is also the only stitch that can be used for a single line of stitches. The single exception is the Half Cross Stitch which is not suitable for mono canvas.

Right-Handed Stitchers work from right to left and top to bottom.

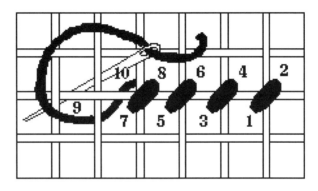

ILLUSTRATION OF RIGHT-HAND CONTINENTAL STITCH

Left-Handed Stitchers work from left to right and bottom to top.

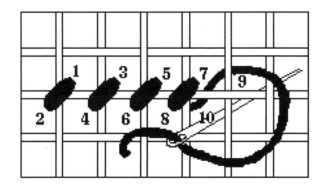

ILLUSTRATION OF LEFT-HAND CONTINENTAL STITCH

Whether left-handed or right-handed, rotate the canvas completely, so that the top becomes the bottom as in the illustrations below. Continue stitching as you did the first row. Remember to rotate your canvas at the end of each row. Note: On your return you will be sewing into a completed row.

The <u>Right-Hand Continental Stitch</u> Illustration shows the first row of right-handed continental stitch and a return row.

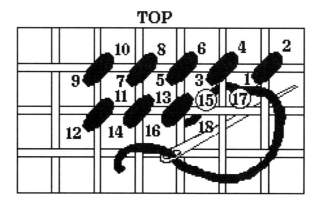

The <u>Left-Hand Continental Stitch</u> Illustration shows the first row of left-handed continental stitch and a return row.

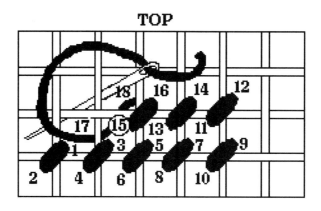

30

Vertical Continental Stitches

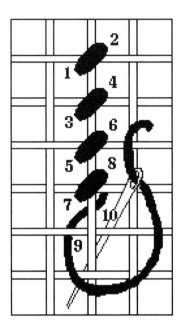

ILLUSTRATION OF RIGHT-HANDED
VERTICAL CONTINENTAL STITCH

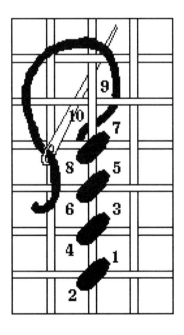

ILLUSTRATION OF LEFT-HANDED
VERTICAL CONTINENTAL STITCH

As the continental stitch warps the canvas a great deal, care must be taken with stitching tension. *This stitch should only be used for working over a single canvas thread and for outlining.*

HALF CROSS STITCH

The Half Cross Stitch is the third Tent Stitch. It is virtually useless to the modern stitcher as it offers no backing and sits poorly on a mono canvas. If you buy a design printed on penelope canvas and plan to use it as a picture, you will find directions for the Half Cross Stitch on the canvas tag. This is the only time you should ever consider using this stitch for a needlepoint project. This stitch looks just like the Continental Stitch but it is stitched left to right by a right-hander instead of right to left. Left-handers stitch right to left. This stitch uses half as much yarn as the other tent stitches and the back looks like little straight stitches which is why it has poor wearability. We DO NOT RECOMMEND the use of this stitch for needlepoint.

TOP

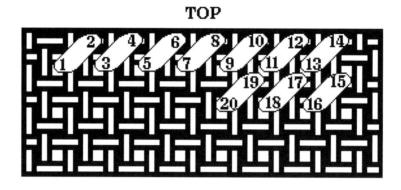

ILLUSTRATION OF RIGHT-HANDED HALF CROSS STITCH

TOP

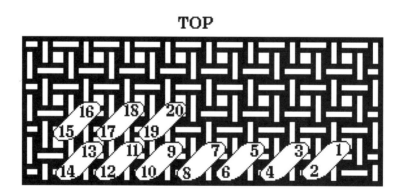

ILLUSTRATION OF LEFT-HANDED HALF CROSS STITCH

32

Straight Stitches

Straight Stitches are what the name implies. They are plain stitches which run either in a vertical or horizontal direction. The differences arise from the way these plain straight **stitches are combined as well as the way they are placed on the canvas. As a general** rule, you need one extra ply of yarn to cover the canvas with any of these stitches. If you are using non- plied yarns such as perle cotton, use the larger size thread. All of these Straight Stitches are excellent for backgrounds and rarely distort the canvas.

Care should be taken to maintain even tension, especially if you are not working on a frame. Except for the darning patterns, these stitches will sit higher on your canvas then tent or diagonal stitches and you should consider this when planning their use. Straight Stitches rarely are yarn hogs and the Darning Stitch is very yarn-saving.

Left-handed instructions for all Straight Stitches: You will feel more comfortable if you turn the diagram top to bottom and begin your stitching in the lower left hand corner. If you are working on a frame this will not be necessary as you will be quite comfortable following the diagrams as they are presented.

BRICK STITCH

The Brick Stitch is an excellent background stitch which offers good backing when done as illustrated in the accompanying diagram. Brick Stitch works up rather quickly and is relatively snagproof when worked over two or four threads. If you elongate the stitch over six or more threads it will snag. These stitches can be worked vertically or horizontally on the canvas. Simply turn the diagram one quarter turn to see the stitch vertically. Brick stitches are easy to compensate around design elements.

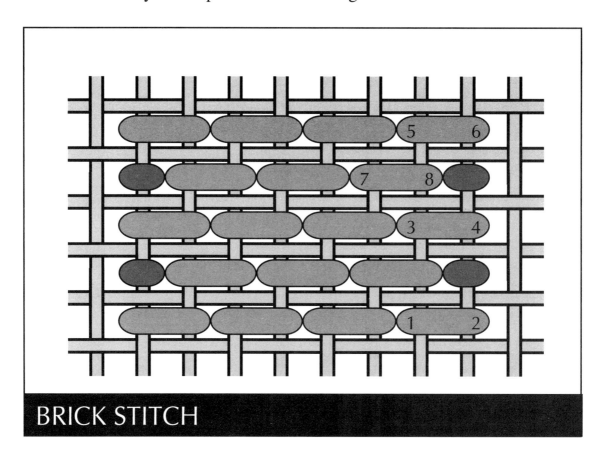

BRICK STITCH

Left-Handed Instructions of Brick Stitch. Turn the diagram top to bottom and begin stitching in the lower left-hand corner.

DOUBLE BRICK STITCH VARIATION

The Double Brick Stitch Variation is an excellent background stitch which offers good backing when done as illustrated in the accompanying diagram. Double Brick Stitch Variation works up rather quickly and is relatively snagproof when worked over two or four threads. If you elongate the stitch over six or more threads it will snag. These stitches can be worked vertically or horizontally on the canvas. Simply turn the diagram one quarter turn to see the stitch vertically. Brick stitches are easy to compensate around design elements.

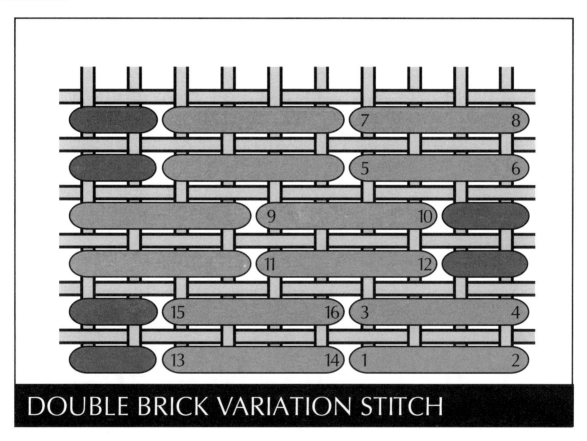

DOUBLE BRICK VARIATION STITCH

Left-Handed instructions for Double Brick Stitch Variation. Turn the diagram top to bottom and begin stitching in the lower left-hand corner.

DARNING PATTERN STITCH

This darning pattern is a very quick to stitch, easily compensated background stitch. Work darning stitches on a frame because the stitch length often causes bowing of the canvas. To avoid excessive warping of your canvas as you change directions, maintain even tension throughout your work. Once you have mastered this simple darning pattern, try long and short stitches and experiment with different colors. You will find design ideas in huck weaving and smocking charts. Darning patterns are more decorative than durable though they use yarn economically. For these reasons, they are better for embellishing than for background stitching.

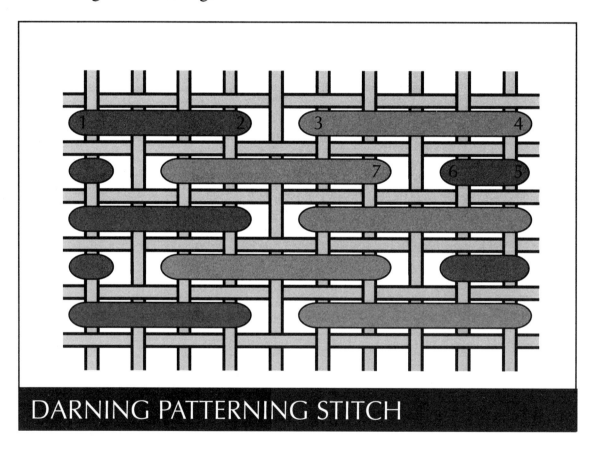

DARNING PATTERNING STITCH

Left-handed instructions for the Darning Pattern Stitch. As this is a weaving technique there are no instructional changes for left-handers.

FLORENTINE STITCH

Florentine or Bargello or Irish Stitches have turned up all over the world and everywhere you find these stitches they are named for the "country of origin." Most Americans call these stitches Bargello but most embroiderers call this Florentine Work. Whatever the name, the charm is from the color selection. If you wish a moire finish choose four or more shades of one color family. If you wish a sharp modern look, choose contrasting colors.

We show you two basic patterns but there are countless others. Combining these two patterns or working either pattern in a mirror image will provide still more variations. Bargello patterns look best when centered on your canvas.

<u>At the end of each row check the peaks to see that they are all on the same thread of canvas. If you find an error, correct it immediately.</u>

Monochomatic bargello patterns make lovely backgrounds. Once the first row is counted in, the stitches work up fast.

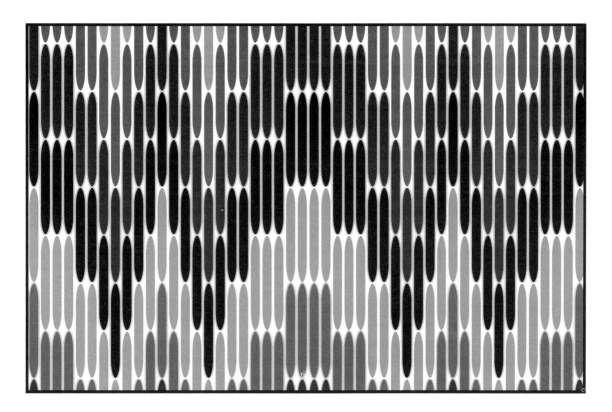

Note: Do not try to conserve wool when stitching Florentine patterns as the padding on the back determines the wearability of the project. Do not pull these stitches too tight as a relaxed tension allows the wool to "bloom" or to spread across the canvas to the full extent of its hand (loft). A relaxed tension will also minimize gaps between the rows.

37

FLORENTINE STITCH PATTERN ONE

This is the basic pointed Florentine patttern. Each stitch covers four threads and each step is up or down two threads. The stitches can be lengthened and the progression up and down can be changed. This will alter your pattern. If your stitches cover more than six threads, your project will snag and not wear as well.

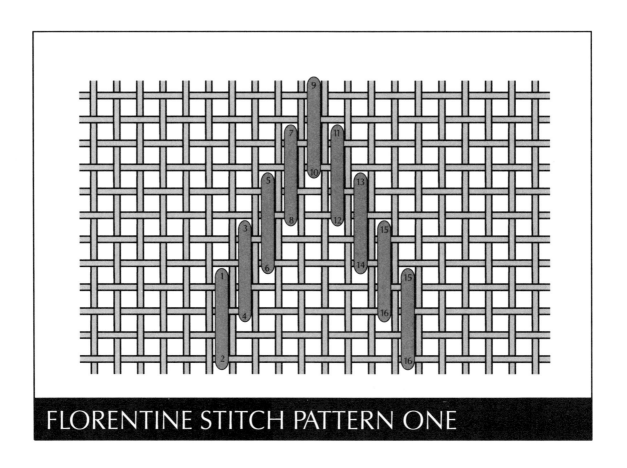

FLORENTINE STITCH PATTERN ONE

Left-handed instructions for all Florentine stitches: You will feel more comfortable if you turn the diagram top to bottom and begin your stitching in the lower left hand corner. If you are working on a frame this will not be necessary as you will be quite comfortable following the diagrams as they are presented.

FLORENTINE STITCH PATTERN TWO

This is the basic rounded Florentine pattern. The difference is that you must observe the count of the stitch groups carefully. If you increase the number of groups your curve will be higher and if you increase the number of stitches per group your curve will be wider. When you work this as a mirror image, you create ovals and diamonds which can be filled with other designs or monograms.

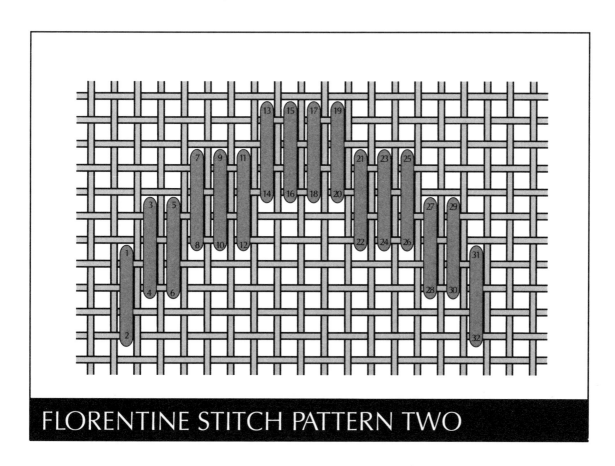

FLORENTINE STITCH PATTERN TWO

When stitching the rounded patterns you will have stitches that are adjacent to each other. If these stitches are rolling away from each other, it is because you have started your new stitch next to the point where you have ended your last one. See illustration one below. Illustration two shows the correct method.

Illustration One

Illustration Two

39

GOBELIN DROIT (UPRIGHT GOBELIN) STITCH

Like the basic tent stitch, Upright Gobelin Stitch is the Basic Straight Stitch. Classic Gobelin Stitch is shown in diagram one. It provides excellent backing, is quick to stitch, and forms a pleasing linear pattern on your canvas. Here is a little experiment to try. Stitch a row of Upright Gobelin Stitch over two threads. Using the same color, stitch a row over five threads. Follow that with a row over three. Notice how the color changes even though you have not changed colors. This is caused by the reflection of light on the different length stitches. Example two shows this stitch worked over a laid thread which can be the same or a contrasting color. Upright Gobelin Stitch over one canvas thread must always be stitched over a laid thread, as in example 3. Examples 4 and 5 show how to corner this stitch. This is useful for framing your design. Try this cornering technique with other straight stitches in this section. As an alternative, you could fill your corners with cross stitches or some of the decorative stitches found elsewhere in this book.

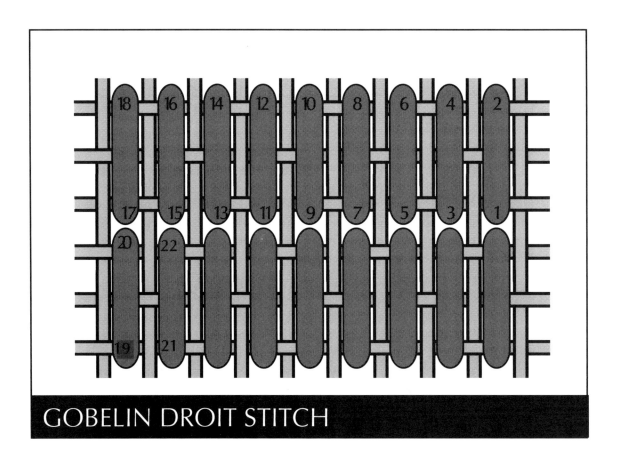

GOBELIN DROIT STITCH

Left-handed instructions for Gobelin stitches: You will feel more comfortable if you turn the diagram top to bottom and begin your stitching in the lower left hand corner. If you are working on a frame this will not be necessary as you will be quite comfortable following the diagrams as they are presented.

HUNGARIAN GROUND STITCH

This stitch is particularly handsome when done in two colors. Work a row of zigzag stitches over four threads and then fill in with the smaller pattern. Study the illustration for placement of the next row of zigzag stitches. This patterned background stitch is quick to work up. It is well padded and relatively snag-proof.

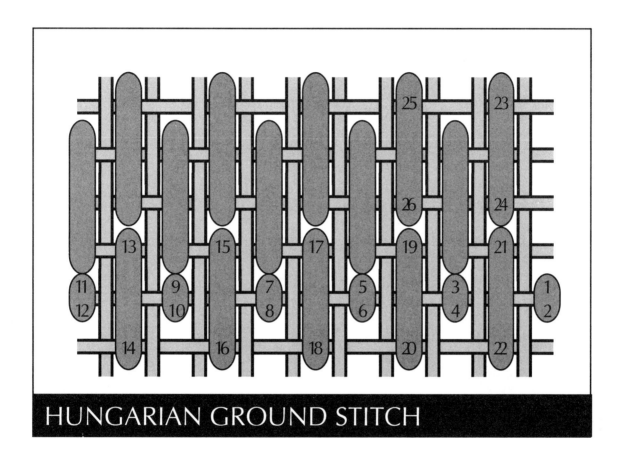

HUNGARIAN GROUND STITCH

Left-handed instructions for Hungarian Ground Stitch. You will feel more comfortable if you turn the diagram top to bottom and begin your stitching in the lower left hand corner. If you are working on a frame this will not be necessary as you will be quite comfortable following the diagrams as they are presented.

VICTORIAN STEP STITCH

The longer stitch has a tendency to snag, especially if this stitch is rescaled to six or eight threads high. It works up more slowly than most of the other straight stitches but gives a pleasing background look with just a slight diagonal striped appearance for texture.

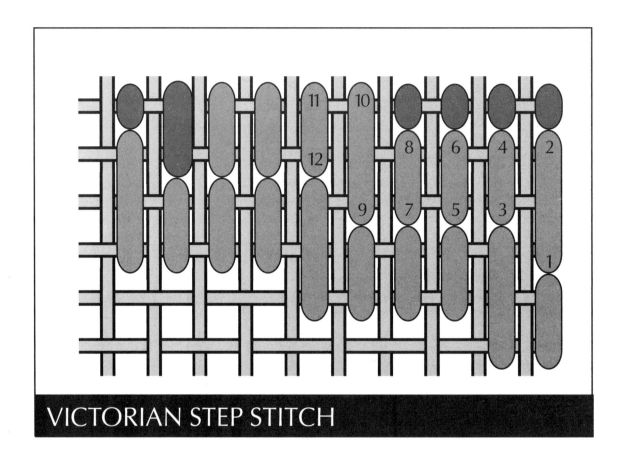

VICTORIAN STEP STITCH

Left-handed instructions for Victorian Step Stitch. You will feel more comfortable if you turn the diagram top to bottom and begin your stitching in the lower left hand corner. If you are working on a frame this will not be necessary as you will be quite comfortable following the diagrams as they are presented.

Diagonal Stitches

Diagonal stitches are worked as the name implies. The tent stitches discussed earlier are the most widely used diagonal stitches. Tent stitches are worked over only one canvas thread. All the stitches in this section are worked over two or more canvas threads. The strong diagonal direction the needle takes across the back of the canvas while creating these stitches causes severe warping. You should work all these stitches on a frame. Left-handed instructions will accompany each stitch.

CASHMERE STITCH

This stitch makes a pattern of little rectangles which provides a pleasing background with good padding. However, it warps the canvas a great deal. Try working this stitch in two colors.

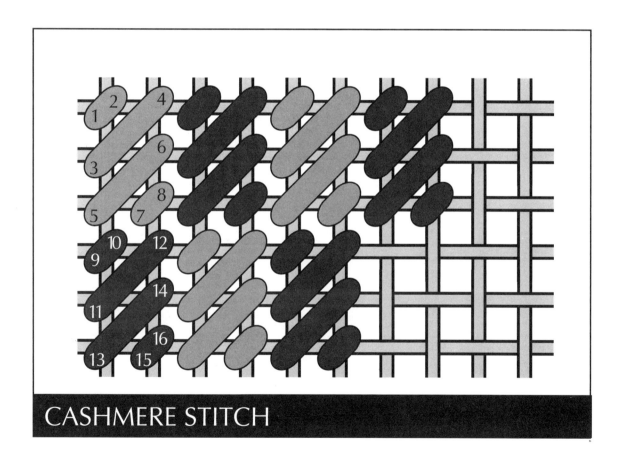

CASHMERE STITCH

Left-handed instructions for Cashmere Stitch. Turn the canvas top to bottom and start at the lower left hand corner. Try working this stitch in two colors. A frame will be very helpful for this stitch.

DIAGONAL OR PLAITED INTERLACED STITCH

A perfect stitch for a piece that will be mounted inside a tray or table top. It offers virtually no padding on the back but is quick to work up and makes a strong textural statement. We worked it in two colors on the diagonal striped sampler in this book. It is one of the few diagonal stitches which does not warp the canvas.

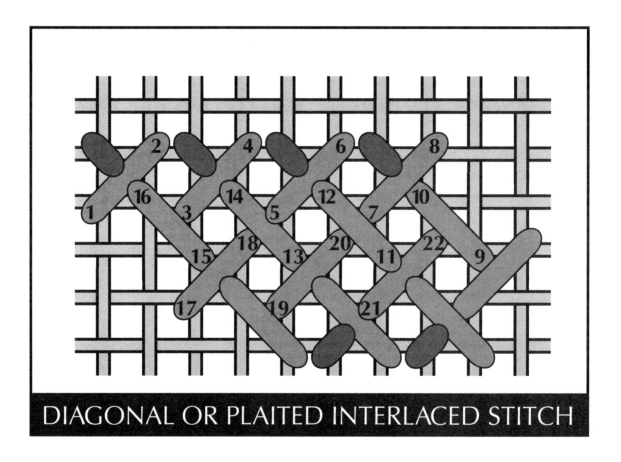

DIAGONAL OR PLAITED INTERLACED STITCH

Left-handed instructions for Diagonal or Plaited Interlaced Stitch. Turn the diagram from top to bottom and begin in the lower left-hand corner as they do for basketweave.

DIAGONAL MOSAIC STITCH

If you follow the suggested stitching method you will find that this stitch will provide good backing, be quick to stitch and cause minimum warping of your canvas. Notice the similarity to basic basketweave which makes this an easily compensated stitch.

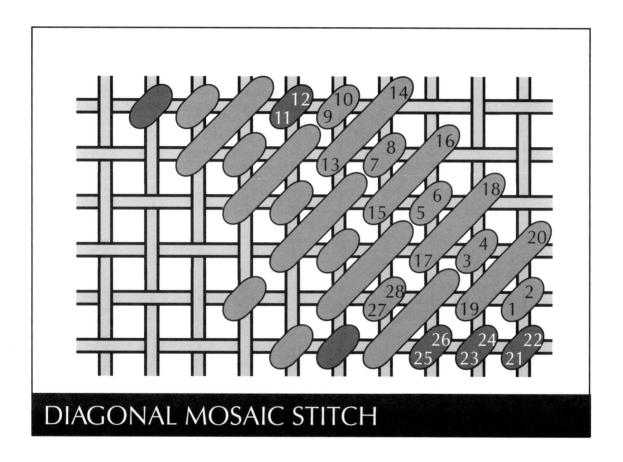

DIAGONAL MOSAIC STITCH

Left-handed Instructions for Diagonal Mosaic Stitch. Turn the diagram from top to bottom and begin in the lower left-hand corner as in basketweave.

DIAGONAL STITCH

The Diagonal Stitch is quick to stitch, well padded on the back, and one of the greatest canvas warpers of them all. We feel that a frame is absolutely necessary for this stitch. The stitch snags easily and you have to watch your tension carefully in order to achieve a smooth appearance. Diagonal Stitch is used in the Diagonal Striped Sampler.

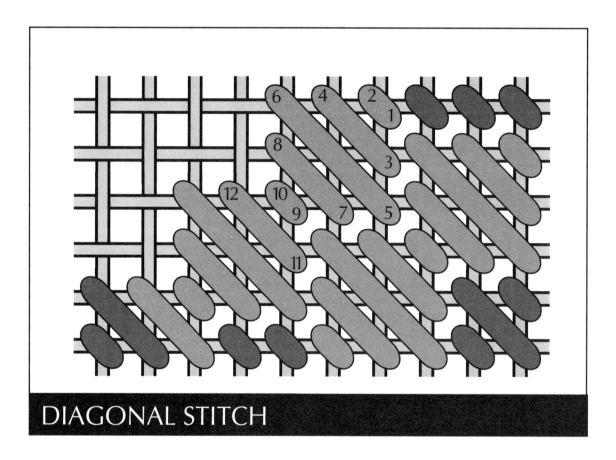

DIAGONAL STITCH

Left-handed instructions for Diagonal Stitch. Turn the diagram from top to bottom and begin in the upper left-hand corner,

GOBELIN STITCH SLANTED

This stitch can be worked left to right like Half Cross Stitch or right to left as Continental Stitch. The Half Cross method will cause less warpage and conserve thread. Both methods are quick to stitch and offer good padding for greater wearability. Like any straight stitch, if rescaled to cover more than four threads, Slanted Gobelin Stitch will snag easily. This stitch can be worked vertically as well as horizontally on the canvas. If you plan to cover large areas of canvas with Slanted Gobelin Stitch you should mount your work on a frame as this stitch distorts the canvas badly. Remember to have maximum coverage on the back which would look similar to continental stitch.

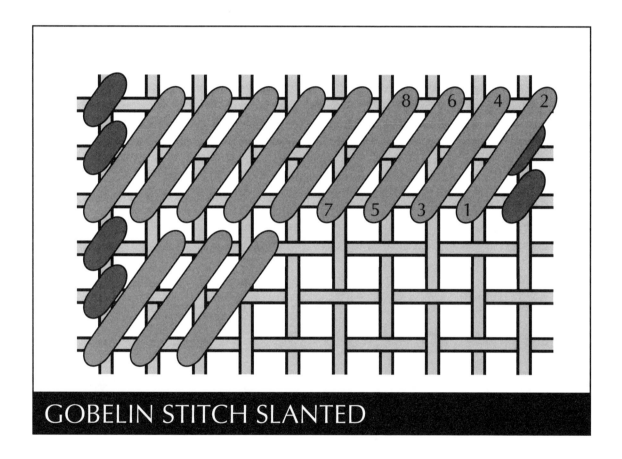

GOBELIN STITCH SLANTED

Left-handed instructions for Gobelin Stitch Slanted. Left handed stitchers can work this stitch in the manner most comfortable to them, However, its similarity to Continental Stitch would argue for its being worked in that manner, left to right across the canvas. Worked as Continental Stitch, it will have maximum coverage on the back. If you plan to cover large areas of canvas with Slanted Gobelin Stitch you should mount your work on a frame as this stitch distorts the canvas badly.

JACQUARD STITCH

Jacquard stitch is a real canvas warper but makes an interestingly patterned background. If worked on a frame your canvas will more likely retain its original shape. If you eliminate the shorter stitches and repeat the others you will be working the Byzantine stitch. Both of these stitches can be rescaled up to five diagonal threads. Jacquard stitch is pretty when done in more than one color. It is a well-padded stitch.

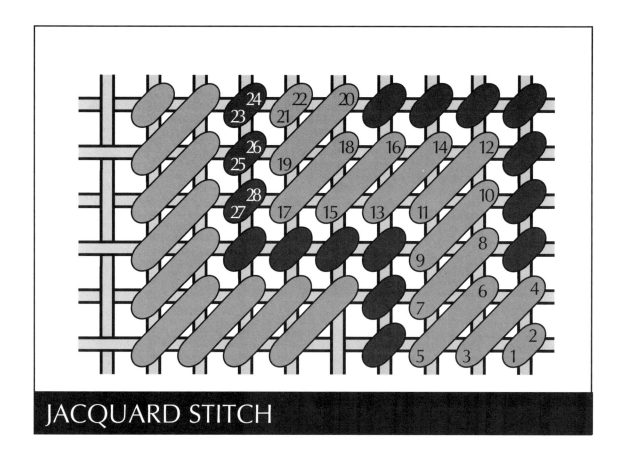

JACQUARD STITCH

Left-handed instructions for Jacquard Stitch. Turn the diagram from top to bottom and begin at lower left corner.

KNITTING STITCH

This is a hard-wearing tight stitch that makes a good filler or background. It uses about the same amount of yarn as basketweave. This stitch fits in narrow areas but can also be rescaled. It looks like its name and is fun to use.

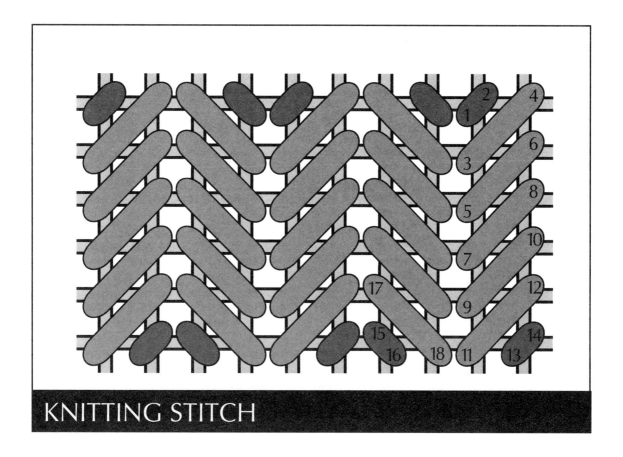

KNITTING STITCH

Left-handed instructions for Knitting Stitch. Reverse this stitch from left to right.

MILANESE STITCH

Here is yet another canvas-warper that should be worked on a frame. Whether worked in one or two colors it forms a striking arrowhead pattern and is worked from the upper left hand corner to the lower right hand corner.

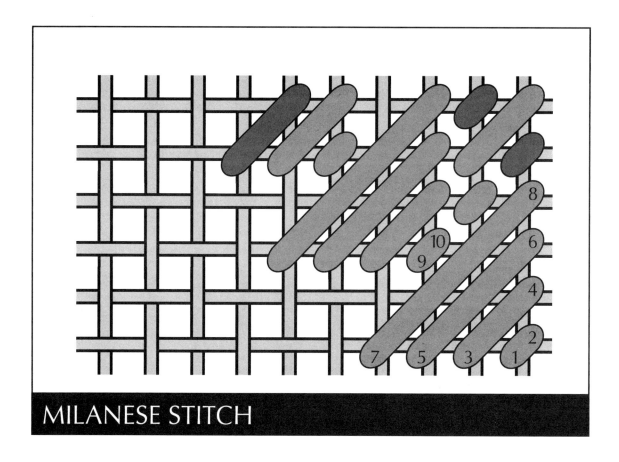

MILANESE STITCH

Left-handed instructions for Milanese Stitch. Turn the diagram from top to bottom and begin in the lower right-hand corner. It will be worked up toward the upper left corner of the rotated diagram.

MOSAIC STITCH

This is an easily compensated background stitch. It is hard-wearing and forms a pleasing texture. Try working it in two colors for a checkerboard effect. **Beware: this stitch is a canvas warper.** If you alternate the direction of the stitch blocks you will minimize the warping and create an alternative pattern. This is the smallest of the family of stitches which form box-like patterns. Others are the Cashmere Stitch and the Scotch Stitch.

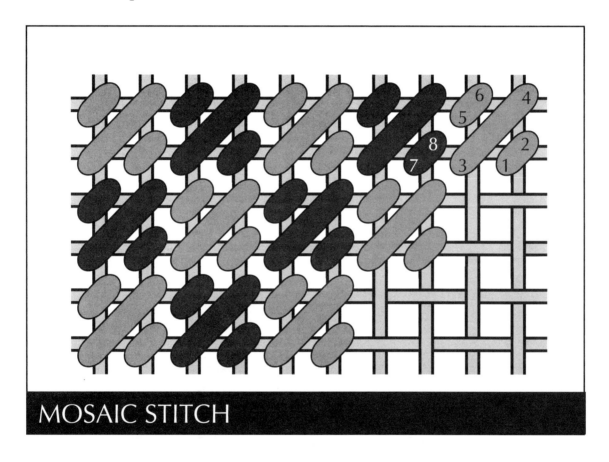

MOSAIC STITCH

Left-handed instructions for Mosaic Stitch. Turn the diagram from top to bottom and begin in the upper left-hand corner.

SCOTCH STITCH

This stitch forms a large square box which makes a good checker board pattern. It is quick to stitch, well padded on the back and is the greatest canvas warper of them all. Work this stitch in the diagonal method as you do the Diagonal Mosaic Stitch. We feel that a frame is absolutely necessary for this stitch. This stitch snags easily and you will have to watch your tension carefully because it is difficult to achieve a smooth surface with this stitch. In spite of all these disclaimers, both authors use this stitch extensively for its appearance. We hope you will too.

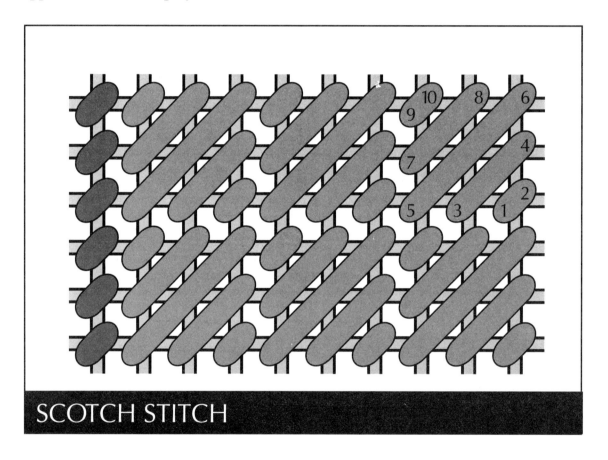

SCOTCH STITCH

Left-handed Instructions for Scotch Stitch. Turn the diagram from top to bottom and begin in the upper left-hand corner.

STEM STITCH

This stitch is composed of alternating rows of diagonal gobelin stitches over any number of diagonal threads. Cover the exposed threads between the two rows with a backstitch. Use a heavier yarn for longer diagonals but do not increase the yarn used for the backstitches. The backstitch is worked last. It is pleasing worked in a different color. This stitch works up fast, especially when elongated and is well padded. The different angles of the stitches reflect the light differently so even when worked monochromatically this stitch has a shaded effect.

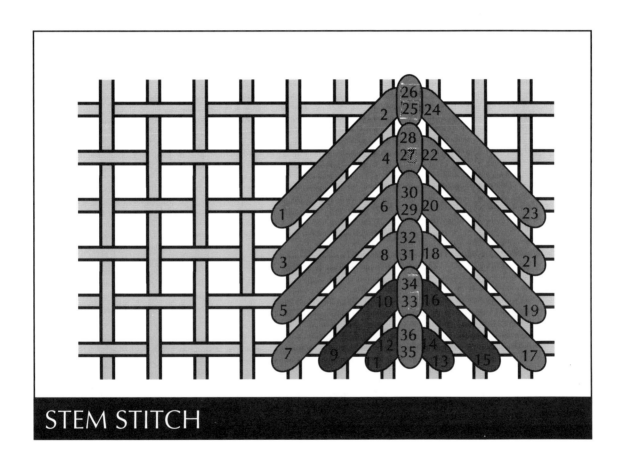

STEM STITCH

Left-handed instructions for Stem Stitch. Reverse left and right on the instructions.

Cross Stitches

According to Katherine Ireys, the French terms *gros point* and *petit point* do not apply to large and small stitches on penelope canvas but to describe the size of a Diagonal Cross Stitch. Each Cross Stitch is made up of two Diagonal Stitches crossing in opposite directions. Two Straight Stitches crossing one another create an Upright Cross Stitch. There is a large family of stitches created from combinations of these Diagonal and Upright Stitches. None of the cross stitches we have chosen for this book will cause canvas distortion.

BINDING STITCH

The Binding Stitch is a variation of the Long-armed Cross Stitch. It is a useful stitch for joining and for finshing canvas. In its completed form it resembles a braid. Note in the diagram that the first step skips three threads of canvas. **From then on it skips two threads.** The stitch is generally worked over two horizontal threads of canvas along a folded edge. The last illustration shows the view from the top of a folded over piece of canvas. If you are using the stitch to join two pieces of canvas, fold the canvas so that you will stitch over one thread of each piece. You will find further suggestions for using the binding stitch in our section on finishing needlework.

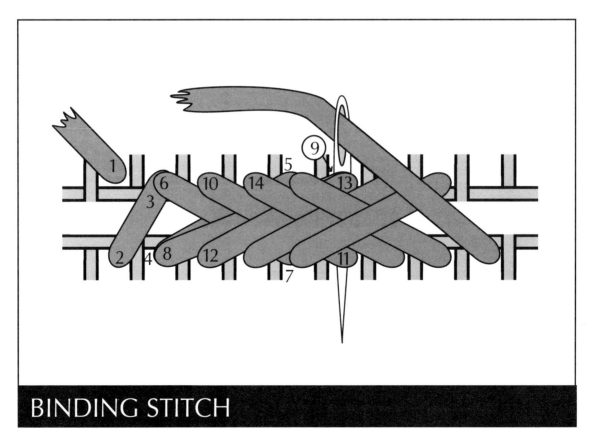

BINDING STITCH

Left-handed instructions for the Binding Stitch. Reverse left and right in the instructions.

CROSS STITCH

The basic cross stitch offers little padding but does not distort the canvas. It is a good accent stitch for eyes, flowers, etc. It is also a good background stitch which works up quickly. It can be stitched as individual units or by making two trips across a row, working half crosses each way. If you will be stitching tiny little cross stitches over only one intersection of mono canvas, the stitch must be worked as a single unit.

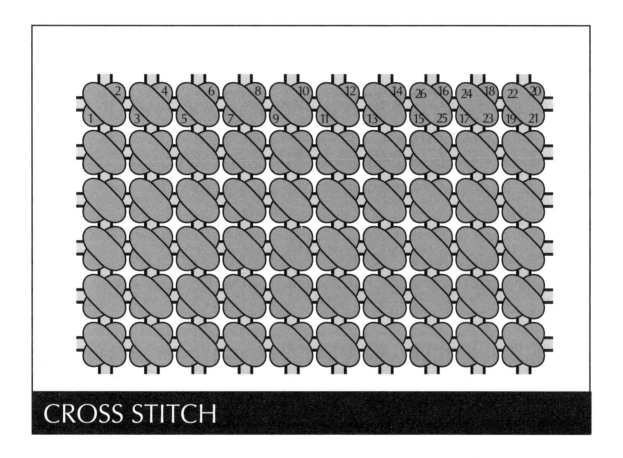

CROSS STITCH

Left-handed instructions for Cross Stitch. Reverse left and right on the instructions.

DOUBLE STRAIGHT CROSS STITCH

This stitch is composed of a large straight cross covered with a smaller diagonal cross. It forms a flower like pattern. The stitch is slow to work up but is firm and hard-wearing in spite of the lack of padding. This stitch makes lovely tree leaves when worked in two shades of green.

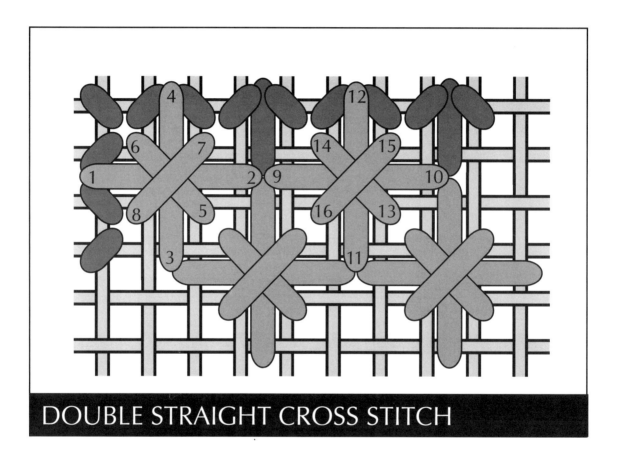

DOUBLE STRAIGHT CROSS STITCH

Left-handed instructions for Double Straight Cross Stitch. Reverse left and right on the instructions.

LEVIATHAN STITCH

This is a decorative stitch that is especially nice in the corners of your borders. It has little padding but when completed as illustrated it is relatively snag-proof. It is a bit slow to work up but fun to stitch. If stitching more than one unit of this stitch, make sure you follow the same sequence of stitches for each leviathan.

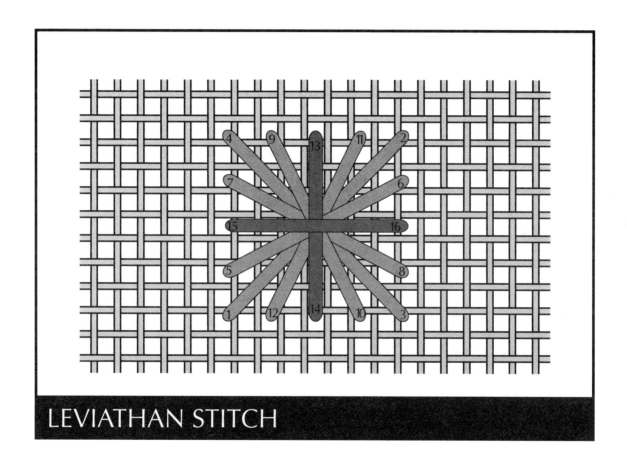

LEVIATHAN STITCH

Left-handed instructions for Leviathan Stitch. Reverse left and right on the instructions.

FERN STITCH

Fern Stitch is worked in vertical rows. When you reach the bottom of the pattern or canvas, compensate your stitches and end your thread. Return to the top to work another row. Do not try to rotate your canvas or you will change the look of this stitch. Backstitching between the rows is a nice finishing touch. Because of its strong texture, this stitch is great for samplers or as an accent in a small area. It is not a choice background stitch since it has little padding and presents a strong design.

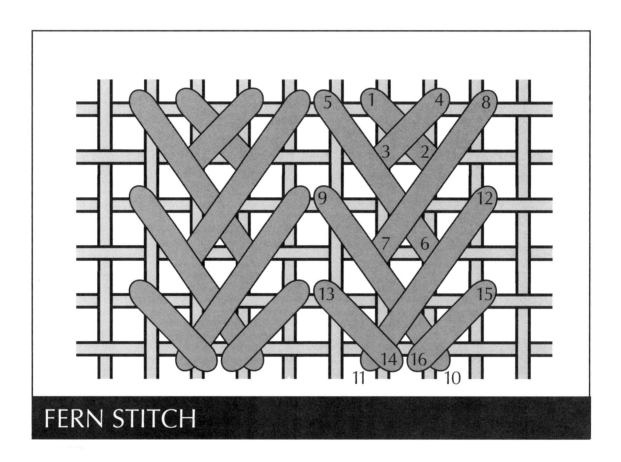

FERN STITCH

Left-handed instructions for Fern Stitch. Reverse left and right on the instructions.

HERRINGBONE STITCH

Herringbone gets its name from the effect produced by the completed stitch. You must not rotate the canvas as you stitch but always work from left to right across the area to be covered. Have the yarn above your hand when proceeding downhill and below your hand when proceeding uphill. This applies to both left and right-handed stitchers. This stitch snags somewhat easily and offers little padding on the reverse. It is quick to stitch and is quite striking worked in one or more colors. Try making a rainbow colored belt. As with all cross stitches, you must be consistent in the direction of your crosses.

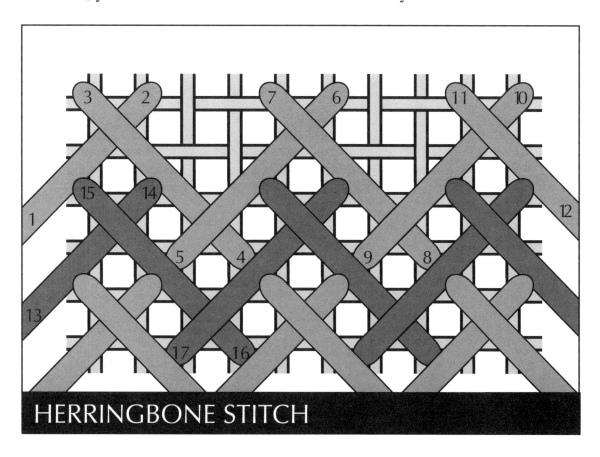

HERRINGBONE STITCH

Left-handed instructions for Herringbone Stitch. Rotate canvas from top to bottom and reverse left and right on the instructions.

59

FOUR-COLOR INTERWOVEN HERRINGBONE STITCH

This is the basic herringbone stitch shown on page 59. On our sampler we have used four colors. You can use any number of colors in an infinite array. If you use the dark color first, it will be easier to see the color transition. Any herringbone stitch can be rescaled. In the advanced sampler, it was rescaled to be worked over six threads.

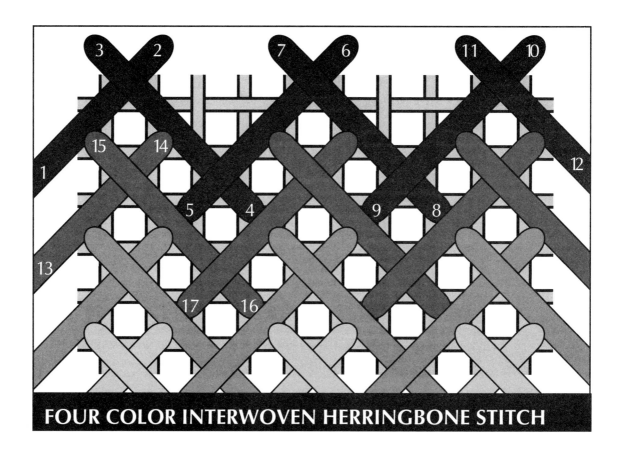

FOUR COLOR INTERWOVEN HERRINGBONE STITCH

Left-handed instructions for Four Color Interwoven Herringbone Stitch. Reverse left and right in the instructions.

HERRINGBONE GONE WRONG STITCH

If you do rotate your canvas while working the herringbone stitch, you will create a pattern called "Herringbone Gone Wrong." It looks like a basket which has been woven on a diagonal. It is an attractive filler stitch. Both herringbone stitches make appealing borders and striking belts. Herringbone stitches work up quickly but offer little padding. They are not recommended for background stitching, especially in irregular areas as the compensation stitches are tedious to count.

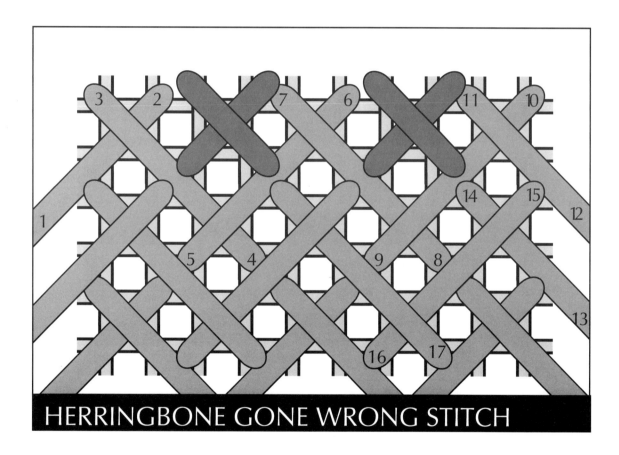

HERRINGBONE GONE WRONG STITCH

Left-handed instructions for Herringbone Gone Wrong Stitch.
Rotate canvas from top to bottom and reverse left and right on the instructions.

DOUBLE LEVIATHAN STITCH

The use of five small upright cross stitches rather than one large upright cross stitch turns the square shape of the Leviathan Stitch into the diamond shape of the Double Leviathan Stitch. It has little padding but when completed as illustrated it is relatively snag-proof. It is a bit slow to work up but fun to stitch. If stitching more than one unit of this stitch, make sure you follow the same sequence of stitches for each leviathan. If you choose to use this stitch for a corner treatment, it will look good when squared off with Basket-weave Stitches.

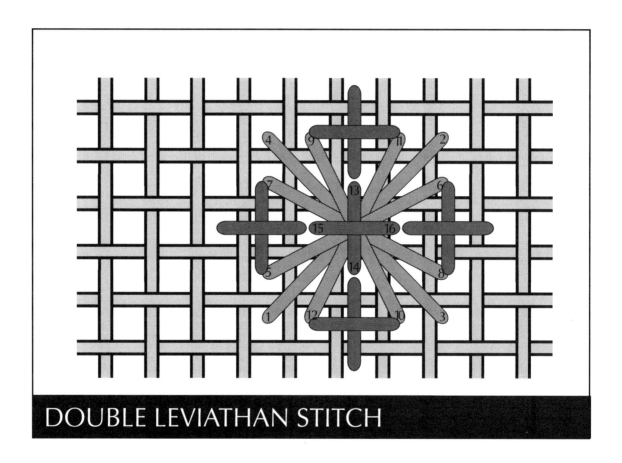

DOUBLE LEVIATHAN STITCH

Left-handed instructions for Double Leviathan Stitch. Reverse left and right on the instructions.

62

LONG-ARMED CROSS STITCH (ALSO KNOWN AS "TVISTØM")

This stitch is also known as Tvistøm, the traditional stitch of Swedish embroidery. It is important to rotate the canvas at the end of each row, making sure that the stitches of each new row line up properly with the stitches of the preceding row. If done correctly, your finished piece will look like rows of tightly woven braid. This is an extremely durable stitch, in spite of its lack of backing. In Sweden, this stitch is used as commonly as we in America use the basketweave stitch. It is quick to work up. The long-armed cross stitch is the basis of the binding stitch.

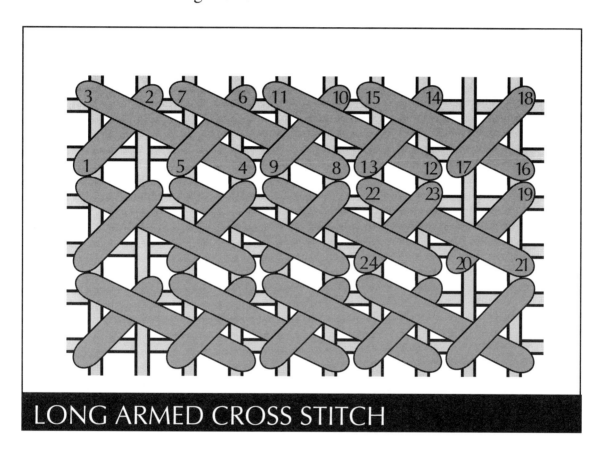

LONG ARMED CROSS STITCH

Left-hand instructions for Long-Armed Cross Stitch. Rotate the canvas from top to bottom and reverse left to right on the directions.

MONTENEGRIN STITCH

This stitch is used in our advanced sampler to separate design elements. It is a variation of the Long-Armed Cross and makes a lovely border. It is easily re-scaled. Change the thickness of your threads for proper canvas coverage. This stitch works up quickly and has a comfortable rhythm.

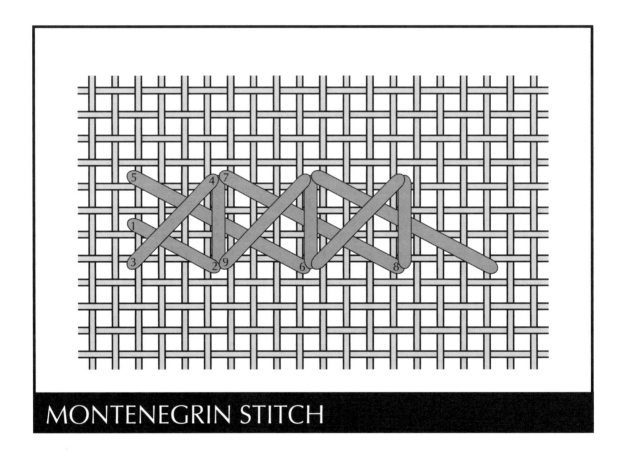

MONTENEGRIN STITCH

Left-handed instructions for Montenegrin Stitch. The rhythm is especially comfortable for the left-handed stitcher. Left-handed stitchers reverse left and right on the instructions.

OBLONG CROSS STITCH WITH BACK STITCH

To conserve yarn, complete each stitch, including the tie down before going on to the next unit. However, if you are using multiple colors, as in the advanced sampler, work all the crossed stitches first and then go back with the second color for the tie-downs. There is no limit to the scale of this stitch as the tie-downs keep it snag-proof and durable. You can create many lovely patterns by varying the colors of the tie-downs.

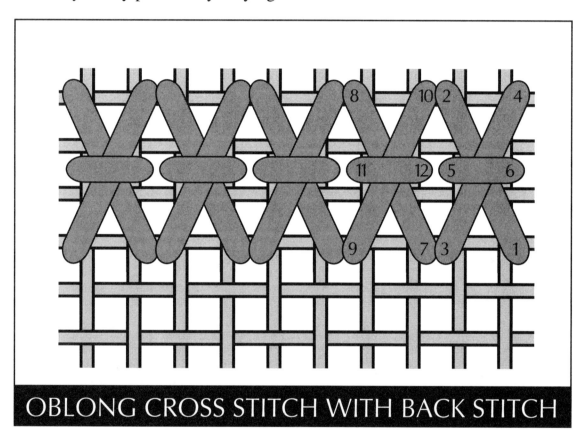

OBLONG CROSS STITCH WITH BACK STITCH

Left-handed instructions for Oblong Cross Stitch with Back Stitch. Reverse left and right on the instructions.

RAISED CROSS STITCH

This is a well-padded, high textured stitch that is easy to rescale. It is a good choice for lending a three-dimensional appearance to bushes and shrubbery.

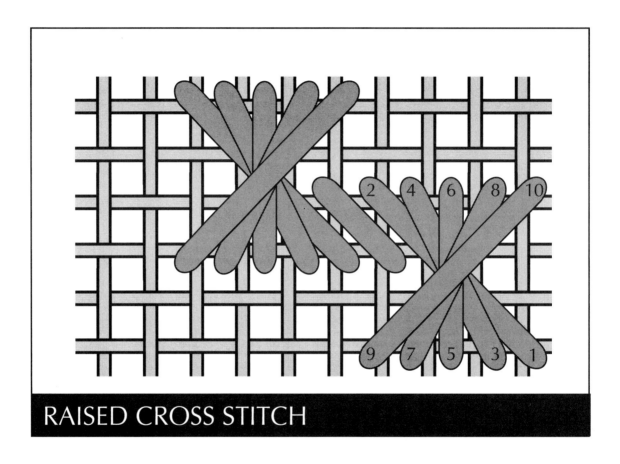

RAISED CROSS STITCH

Left-handed instructions for Raised Cross Stitch. Reverse left and right on the instructions.

REVERSE TVISTØM KNITTING VARIATION STITCH

This is an unusual way of doing a Knitting Stitch. It creates a long-wearing surface which looks exactly like the stockinette stitch in knitting. It can be worked in either vertical or horizontal rows. Be sure to rotate your canvas at the end of each row.

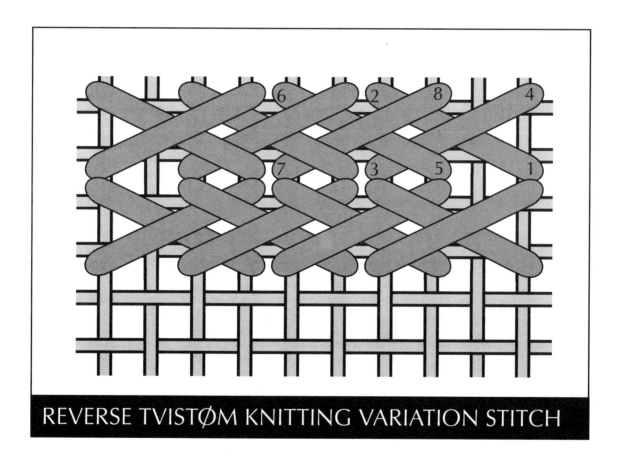

REVERSE TVISTØM KNITTING VARIATION STITCH

Left-handed instructions for Reverse Tvistøm Stitch. Reverse left and right on the instructions.

RHODES STITCH

This stitch was developed by renowned embroiderer Mary Rhodes. It is a lovely decorative stitch which may be used much as the Leviathan Stitch. There is little backing but it is well padded. This stitch can be scaled from three by three threads to nearly any number. However, if working over sixteen or more canvas threads, you should tie down the corners. Note that you must work over an even number of canvas threads if you will need to tie down the corners. The tie downs will be worked from center hole to center hole around the stitch.

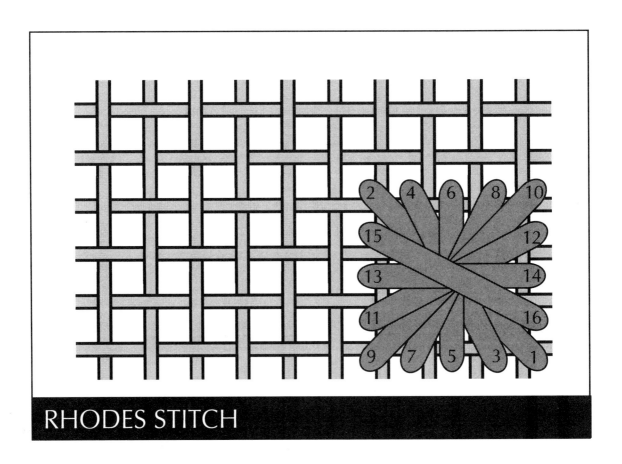

RHODES STITCH

Left-handed instructions for the Rhodes Stitch. Reverse left and right on the instructions.

RICE STITCH OR WILLIAM AND MARY STITCH

Also known as Crossed Corners Stitch, this is a stitch often found in period works, as it has long been a favorite of needleworkers. It works up quickly,forms a strong surface, is well padded on the back. By varying the colors, it is possible to work a field of flowers using just this stitch.

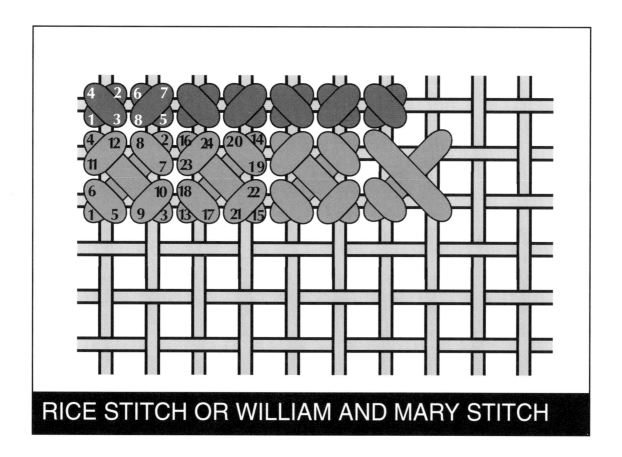

RICE STITCH OR WILLIAM AND MARY STITCH

Left-handed instructions for Rice Stitch. Reverse left and right on the instructions.

RICE STITCH VARIATION

This variation is found on the advanced sampler and has been included to show you how easy it is to rescale stitches.

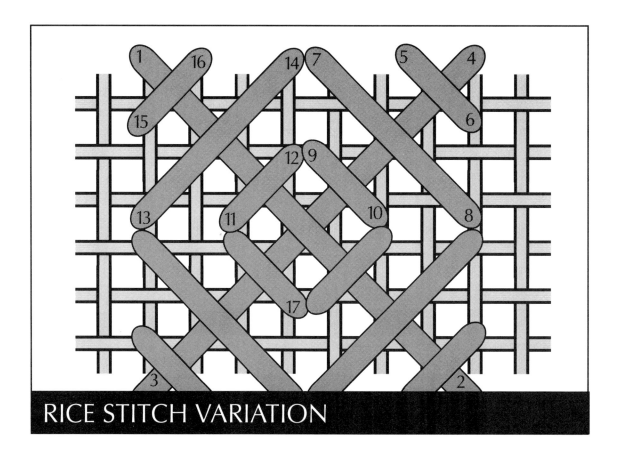

RICE STITCH VARIATION

Left-handed instructions for Rice Stitch Variation. Reverse left and right on the instructions.

SMYRNA CROSS STITCH

This stitch is perfect for animal eyes, polka dots or any round design on your canvas. It also creates a wonderful textured background. The texture simulates the leaves on bushes or trees. Smyrna Stitch does not work up quickly but is fun to do. This is a strong stitch but its high profile causes it to wear sooner than other stitches on the same item.

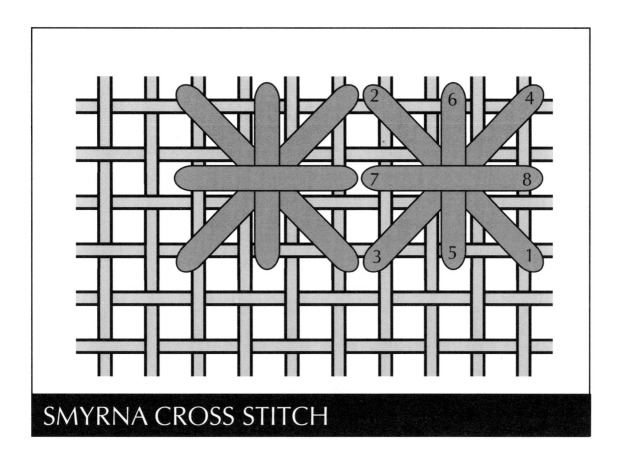

SMYRNA CROSS STITCH

Left-handed instructions for Smyrna Cross Stitch. Reverse left and right on the instructions.

STRAIGHT CROSS STITCH or UPRIGHT CROSS STITCH

As the name implies this cross is composed of two Straight Stitches. It is moderately padded on the back and relatively snag-proof. This is an excellent textured stitch and can easily be rescaled. If you enlarge the stitch, you will need to experiment with the yarn thickness for good canvas coverage.

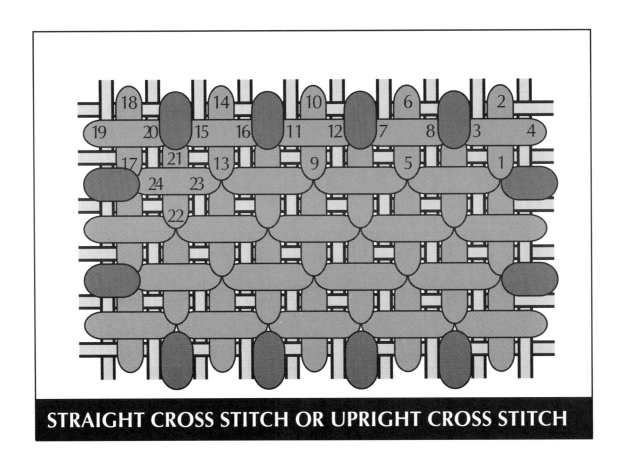

STRAIGHT CROSS STITCH OR UPRIGHT CROSS STITCH

Left-handed instructions for Straight Cross Stitch. Reverse left and right on the instructions.

VAN DYKE STITCH

This stitch is worked in vertical rows which form a braided pattern. It is excellent for narrow areas but is also easily rescaled. It is well-padded in its small version but less so when the stitch is enlarged. It is quick to work up. This stitch uses a great deal of yarn. Stitch a swatch to determine your yarn needs.

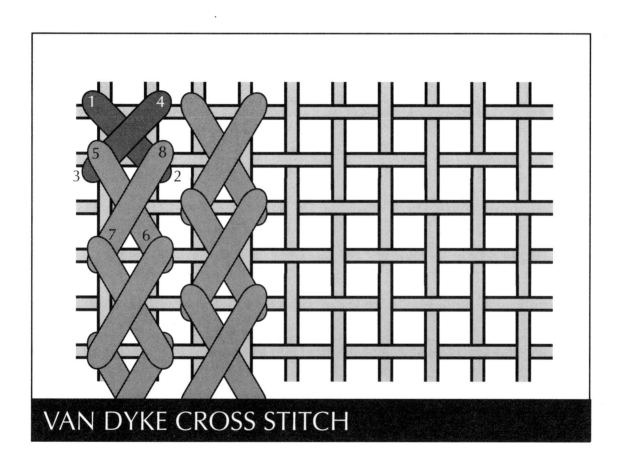

VAN DYKE CROSS STITCH

Left-handed instructions for Van Dyke Stitch. Reverse left and right on the instructions. Be sure to work a sample to test yarn thickness needed and amount used per square inch.

WAFFLE STITCH

Like the Rhodes and Leviathan Stitches, this is an excellent accent stitch. It too may be rescaled but must always be worked over an odd number of threads. Try working it in more than one color or in one of the popular variegated or over-dyed threads. It is relatively snag-proof and hard-wearing but has an uneven backing.

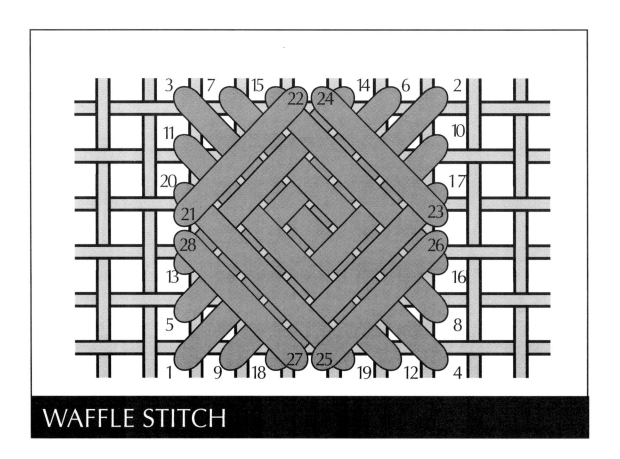

WAFFLE STITCH

Left-handed instructions for the Waffle Stitch. Reverse left and right on the diagram.

**RUGS, MONOGRAMMED
WALL DECOR AND PILLOWS**

B

**NEEDLEPOINT DOOR STOPS
OR BOOKENDS**

**UPSCALE POCKETBOOKS
FOR SPORT OR FORMAL**

C

**ANIMAL PILLOWS ARE FUN TO DO
THEY ADD SO MUCH TO ANY ROOM**

**BELTS, PURSES, AND POCKETBOOK ACCESSORIES
ALL IN NEEDLEPOINT**

D

**PILLOWS-SQUARE OR SHAPED-
DRAGONS, MAN ON THE MOON OR FUNKY FLAMINGOS**

THE PERFECT FORMAL LIVING ROOM SETTING
WITH NEEDLEPOINT

F

**SAMPLER PILLOWS
FOR HOME DECOR**

**PERSONALIZED
CHRISTMAS
STOCKINGS**

G

**FANCY FLOWERS AND FINISHING
MAKE THE PERFECT NEEDLEPOINT PILLOW**

**NEEDLEPOINT RUGS, WALL HANGINGS AND PICTURES
THE PERFECT ROOM ACCENT**

H

**NEEDLEPOINT JUNGLE ANIMALS
FINISHED IN PILLOWS
WITH COORDINATING FAUX FUR FINISH**

Tied Stitches

Tied stitches are generally slow to work up yet very strong and durable. They are always pretty, and many are useful for shading purposes. Any of them will add a touch of originality to your work.

KNOTTED STITCH OVER FIVE THREADS

This is a classic tied down stitch that is very strong and can easily be rescaled. Unlike most tied stitches this one works up rather quickly and is an excellent backgound or filler stitch.

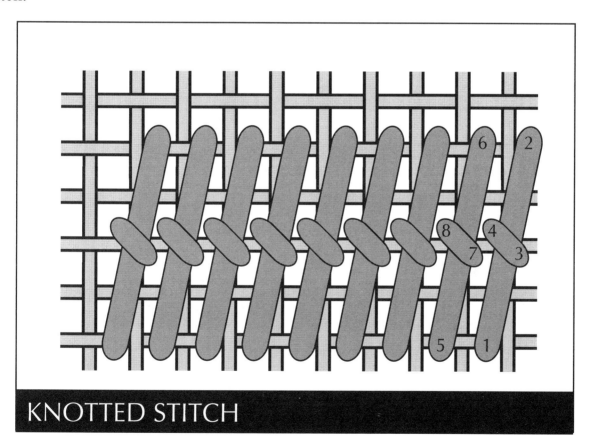

KNOTTED STITCH

Left-handed instructions for Knotted Stitch Over Five Threads. Rotate the canvas top to bottom and work from the lower left corner.

LOOP STITCH

The secret of this stitch is in the tension. Because this stitch is looped rather than tied, you must carefully pull and hold the loop while you are making the next stitch. You will quickly develop the rhythm of this stitch and will like the lacey effect of the little loops riding on top of the long stitch. This stitch was developed from the Buttonhole Stitch family. If the loops are crooked at the end of the row, push them with a fingernail until they are even. When completed as shown, this stitch is hard-wearing and well padded on the back.

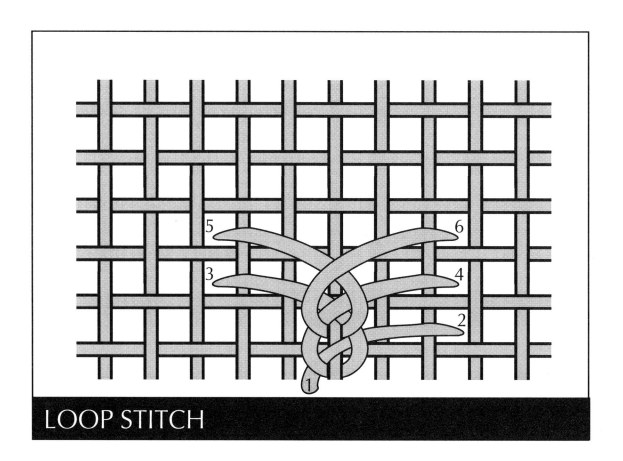

LOOP STITCH

Left-handed instructions for Loop Stitch. Rotate the canvas top to bottom and work from the lower left corner.

LOOPED AND TIED SHEAF STITCH OR SHELL STITCH

This stitch is a combination of four Upright Gobelin Stitches drawn together in the middle by a Horizontal Tie Down Stitch. Pulling your upright stitches too tight will draw together the horizontal threads of the canvas and cause gaps between rows. Be sure to leave the last Upright Gobelin Stitch rather loose to facilitate the tying. The little loops that join the sheaths are worked after a row of sheaths is completed. They are simply woven through the tie downs, first in one direction, then in the reverse. This stitch is quick to work up, does not distort the canvas, and is very well padded.

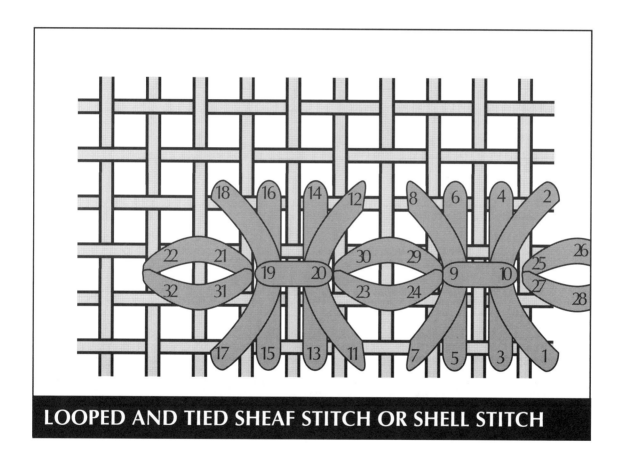

LOOPED AND TIED SHEAF STITCH OR SHELL STITCH

Left-handed instrucitons for Looped and Tied Sheaf Stitch or Shell Stitch. Reverse left and right in the directions.

RENAISSANCE ROCOCCO STITCH

This is a small scaled tightly tied down stitch that is very slow to work up. It is a good accent stitch. It wears very well and would be excellent for stitching small items that are subject to hard wear. Victorians used this stitch for making reticules. Many fine examples can be found in museums.

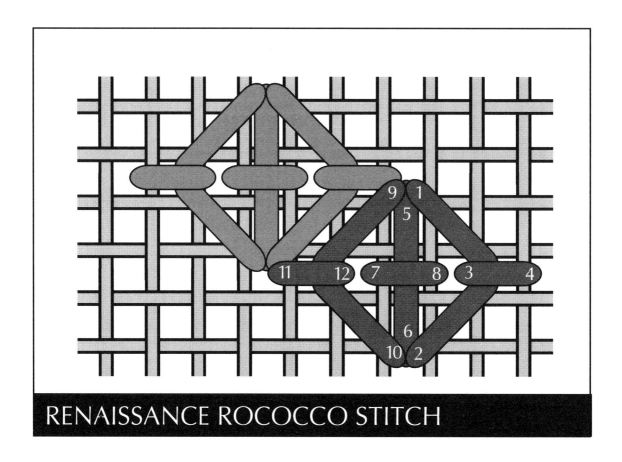

RENAISSANCE ROCOCCO STITCH

Left-handed instructions for Renaissance Rococo Stitch. Rotate the canvas from top to bottom and work from the lower left corner.

78

ROCOCCO STITCH

This stitch is very very slow to work up. It is relatively snag-proof but not well padded on the back. Pay close attention to the numbers on the diagram when learning this stitch. Be sure that you maintain even tension throughout the entire procedure. It must be worked in diagonal lines when doing more than one unit of this stitch.

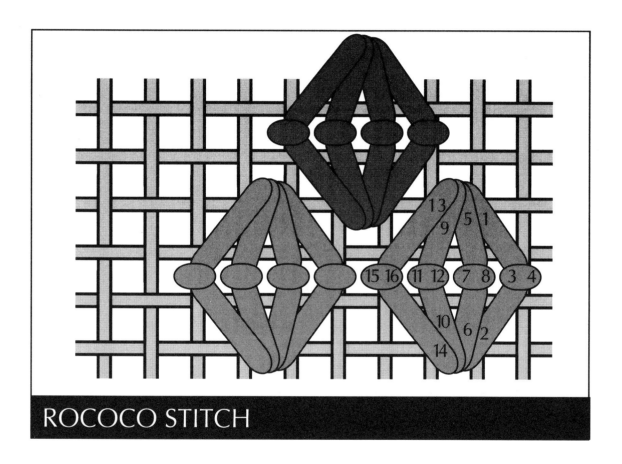

ROCOCO STITCH

Left-handed instructions for Rococco Stitch. Rotate the canvas top to bottom and work from the lower left corner.

GIANT ROCOCCO STITCH

This is simply an enlarged version of the standard Rococco Stitch. It is used on our advanced sampler.

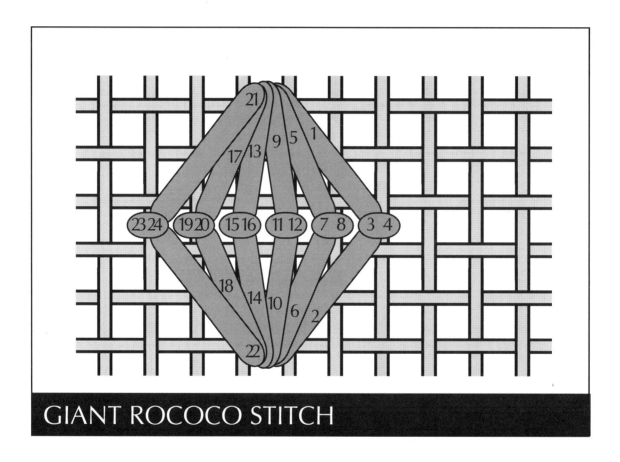

GIANT ROCOCO STITCH

Left-handed instructions for the Giant Rococco Stitch. Rotate the canvas top to bottom and work from the lower left corner.

SHEAF STITCH

This stitch is identical to the Shell Stitch except that the Filler Stitches are Tall Upright **Cross Stitches**. The Sheaf Stitch should be tied more tightly than the Shell Stitch in order to show off the Cross Stitch, which is effective when worked in a second color.

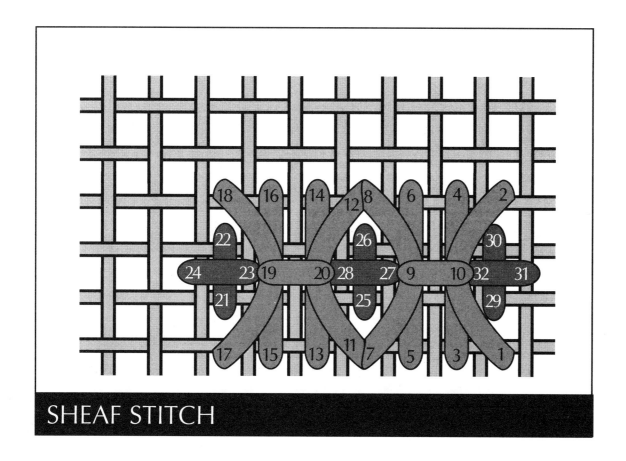

SHEAF STITCH

Left-handed instructions for the Sheaf Stitch. Reverse left and right in the diagram.

STEPPED SHEAF GROUND STITCH

Follow the numbering carefully for this variation of the Sheaf Stitch. Using this stitch sequence makes it an ideal background stitch. In the advanced sampler, the spaces at the top and bottom were not compensated but were filled with Scotch Stitches and Raised Cross Stitches. This stitch is rather quick to work up.

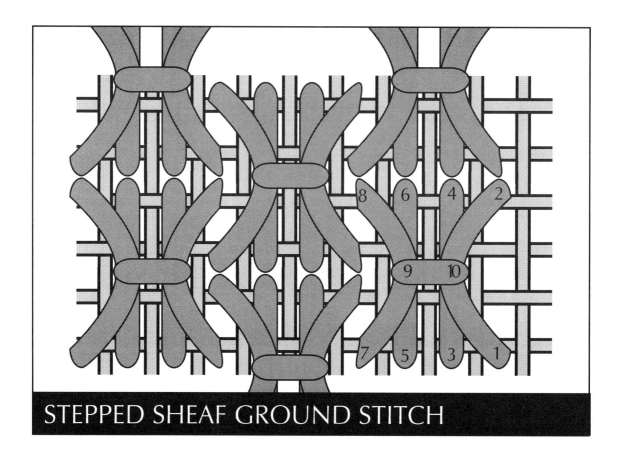

STEPPED SHEAF GROUND STITCH

Left-handed instructions for Stepped Sheaf Ground Stitch. Rotate the canvas top to bottom and work from the lower left corner.

WEB STITCH

This stitch works up fast. It is an attractive background stitch. However, it has no padding and does not wear well. It is snagproof when completed. There is no limit to the length of the stitch to be tied down. When working in an odd-shaped area, be sure to count the threads very carefully on the long stitch in order to have it work out evenly. Notice that all the crosses or ties are two threads to the side and two threads up or down depending on whether the stitcher is right or left-handed.

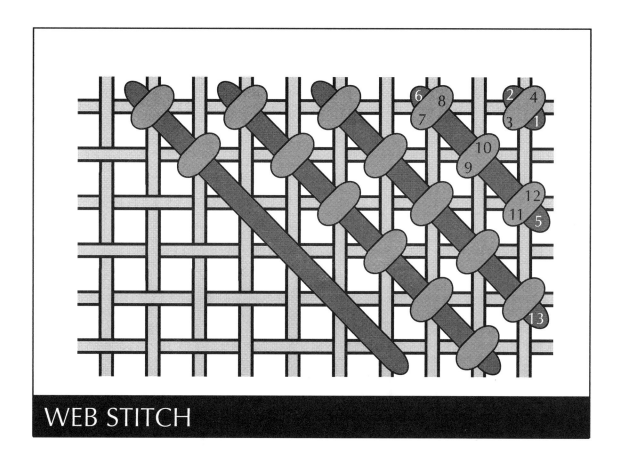

WEB STITCH

Left-handed instructions for the Web Stitch. Rotate the diagram one- quarter turn counter clockwise, and work from the upper left corner.

The trick to most decorative stitches is the tension. In the case of Eyelet Stitches, it is most important to always work from the outside of the stitch to the inside. The tighter your stitches, the larger the Eyelet you will create. These stitches will look better when done with single strands of yarn. If a multi-stranded yarn is chosen, be very careful with your tension. Most of these stitches can also be worked on interlock canvas but those worked with a pulled canvas technique such as the Eyelet Stitches will look much better on Mono Canvas.

ALGERIAN EYELET OR STAR STITCH

This stitch creates a lacey background. It is also an excellent accent stitch. It is slow to work up but is very strong and durable. It is virtually snag-proof. This stitch uses a lot of yarn.

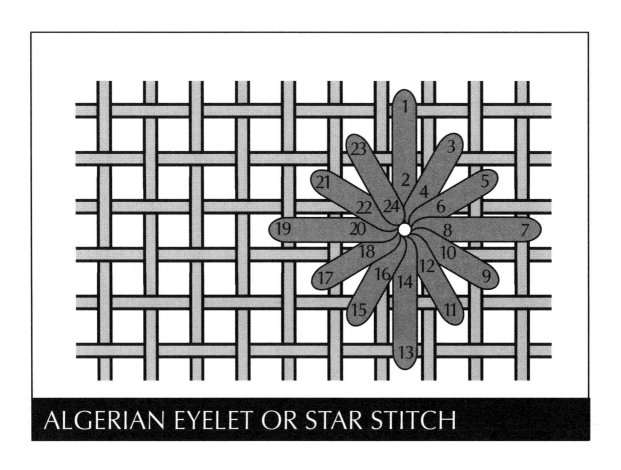

ALGERIAN EYELET OR STAR STITCH

Left-handed instructions for Algerian Eyelet or Star Stitch. Rotate the canvas and begin at the lower left corner. Left-handers will want to work counter-clockwise.

ALGERIAN EYELET VARIATION STITCH

This is a larger variation of the Basic Algerian Eyelet or Star Stitch. It is worked in the same stitch sequence. (See page 84.)

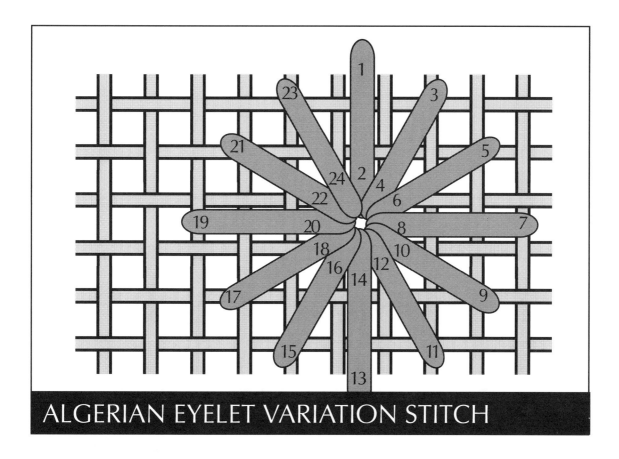

ALGERIAN EYELET VARIATION STITCH

Left-handed instructions for Algerian Eyelet Variation. Rotate the canvas and begin at the lower left corner. Left-handed stitchers will want to work counter-clockwise.

BUTTONHOLE STITCH

Even tension is what makes this stitch look good. It is virtually impossible to create even Buttonhole Stitches without a frame. It does not use much yarn, nor does it wear well as it has virtually no padding on the back.

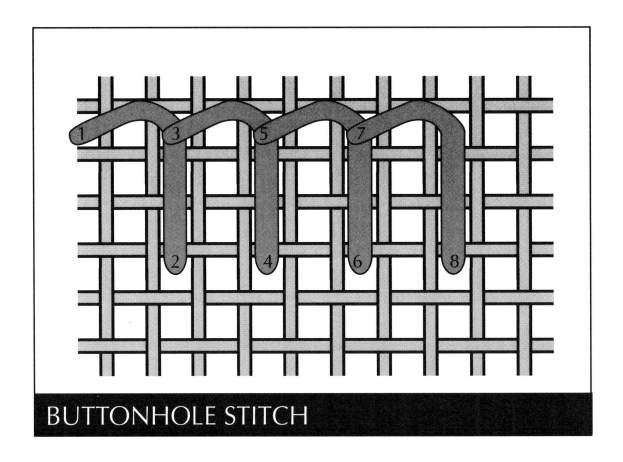

BUTTONHOLE STITCH

Left-handed instructions for Buttonhole Stitch. Left-handed stitchers working on a frame should follow the diagram as presented. If you are not working on a frame, reverse left and right.

BUTTONHOLE BARS STITCH

You must work this stitch on a frame. First work long Straight Stitches in the same or contrasting color. Your Buttonhole Stitches will be stitched over this laid ground. This stitch is well-padded on the front but has virtually no backing. It doesn't distort the canvas and is not snag-proof. It is quick to work up and economical in thread use. It makes very nice borders. When working Buttonhole Stitches, you will want to use longer yarn than usual as it is difficult to neatly change threads. If you must change threads in the middle of the stitch, let the used thread dangle on the back of the canvas, bring your new thread up in the next hole in the stitch sequence while holding both the new and old threads straight down to create the proper tension. After you have completed a few stitches, both tails will need to be woven in to the back.

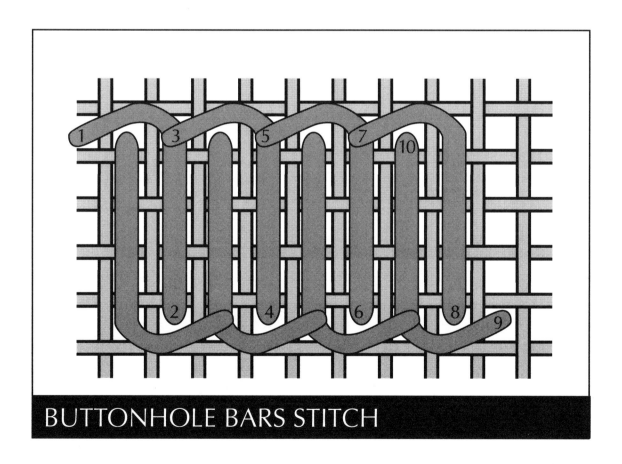

BUTTONHOLE BARS STITCH

Left-handed instructions for Buttonhole Bar Stitch. Work on a frame and follow the diagram as presented.

CHAIN STITCH

This is the one stitch that can go anywhere on your canvas, in any direction, even in a curved path. Chain Stitch is fast to work and quite strong. Remember to leave a channel for it and work the other areas around it first. Even tension is a must on this stitch. If you are going to work this stitch around a tight corner, you will need to tie it down with tiny fastening stitches to maintain the sharp angle. You embroiderers will remember the Lazy Daisy Stitch. This is a series of Chain Stitches originating from the same canvas hole and arranged in flower petal pattern. These Lazy Daisies look very pretty worked over a background of Tent Stitches. We do not think it is pleasing as a background stitch but you might disagree. Stitch a sample and see what you think.

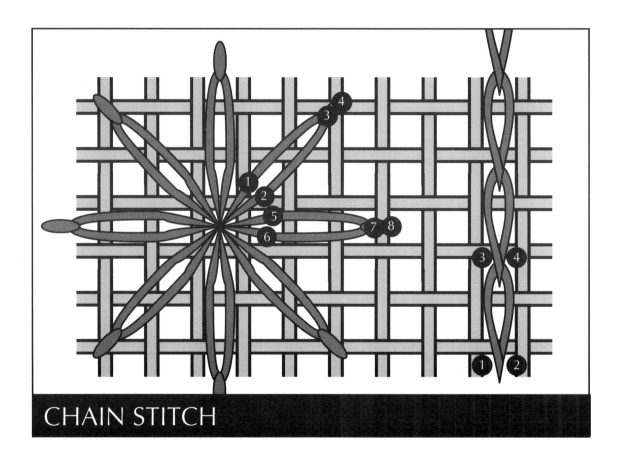

CHAIN STITCH

Left-handed instructions for Chain Stitch. Follow the diagram as presented.

DIAGONAL BUTTONHOLE STITCH

The only trick to this stitch is to make sure your starting stitches and ending stitches all work up a proper diagonal path. This stitch has virtually no backing. It doesn't distort the canvas but is easily snagged. It is quick to work up and economical in thread use. Diagonal Buttonhole Stitch should be worked on a frame, whether right or left-handed.

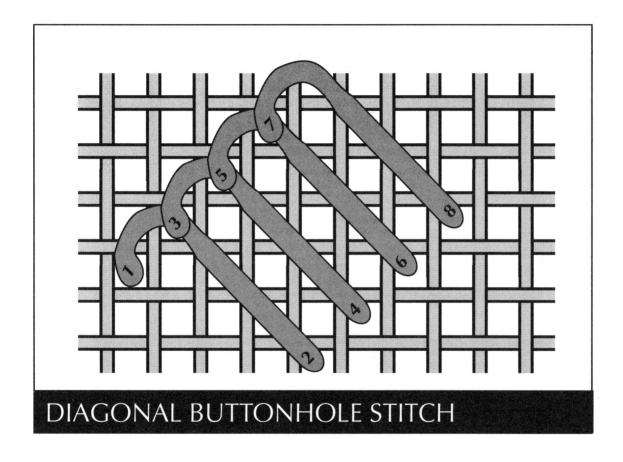

DIAGONAL BUTTONHOLE STITCH

Left-handed instructions for Diagonal Buttonhole Stitch. Rotate the diagram one quarter turn counter clockwise and follow the diagram as presented. A frame is absolutely necessary.

DIAGONAL LEAF STITCH

Diagonal Leaf Stitch may be worked as shown in our diagram but it is also interesting to combine four leaves around one central point so that they form a flower shape. The Leaf Stitch is well-padded and relatively snag-proof. This stitch uses about the same amount of yarn as Basketweave Stitch. It is slow to work up and its definite pattern makes it unsuitable for most backgrounds.

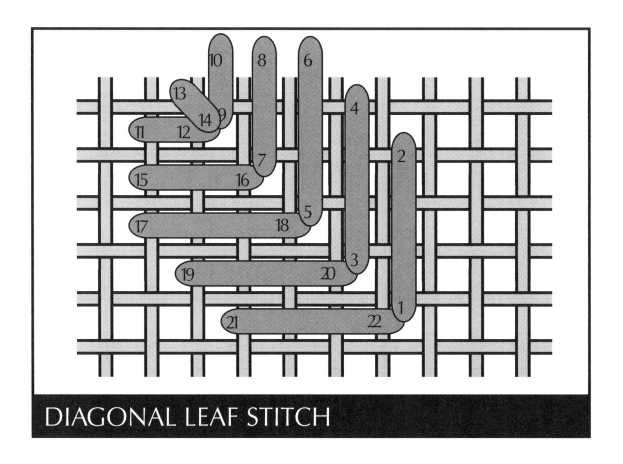

DIAGONAL LEAF STITCH

Left-handed instructions for the Leaf Stitch. Rotate the diagram one quarter turn counter clockwise and follow the diagram as presented.

DIAMOND EYELET STITCH

This is a well-padded, durable stitch. This makes a busy background but is rather slow to work up. If you are making more than one Eyelet Stitch, it would be easier if you stitch in this sequence: complete the top half of each stitch across the row and then complete the bottom half on the return. Be sure to use medium weight yarn and pull your stitches tight. If your yarn is too thin it will not cover the outer portion of the diamond adequately. This stitch uses a lot of thread.

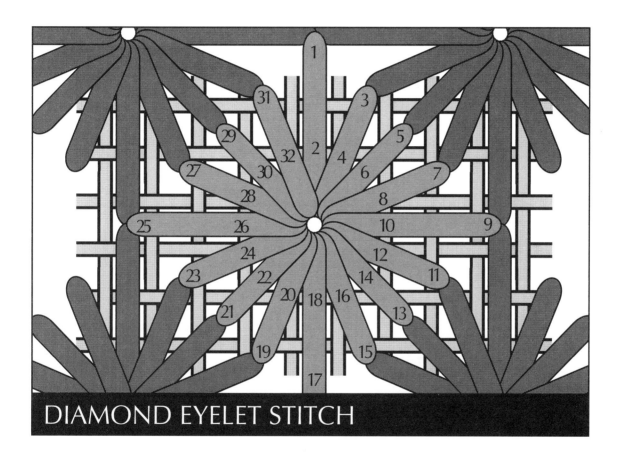

Left-handed instructions for the Diamond Eyelet Stitch. Left-handers will want to work counter-clockwise. Working from right to left, complete the bottom half of each stitch across the row and then complete the top half on the return.

FRENCH KNOT

Using finer yarn than for Tent Stitch, you begin this stitch as if you were making a Tent Stitch. Hold the eye of the needle in your right hand and wind the yarn around the needle once or twice toward the point of the needle. Insert the needle as if you were completing the Tent Stitch and hold it at a right angle to the canvas. With your left hand, pull the yarn, still twisted around the needle, until it is taut. Continue holding the yarn while pushing the needle through with your right hand. When the needle has been pushed through to the back of the canvas, pull the yarn snug. Bunches of these knots make a nubby surface and are wonderful for stitching the hair on curly-headed children, little French poodles, or the foam on top of waves.

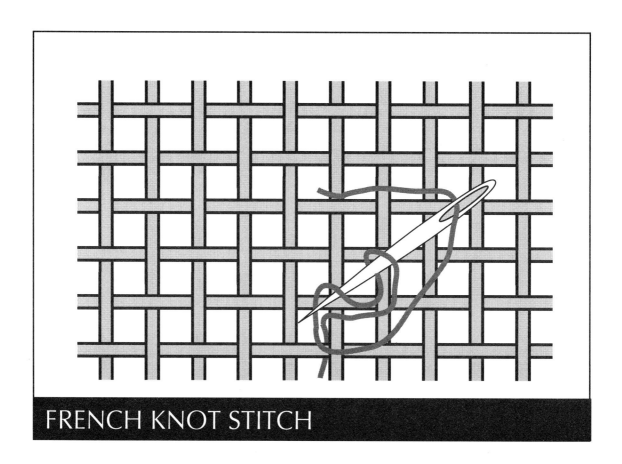

FRENCH KNOT STITCH

Left-handed instructions for the French Knot. Reverse left and right in these directions. For example, hold the needle in the left hand and wrap the yarn with the right hand.

LEAF STITCH

Everything said about the Diagonal Leaf Stitch applies to this stitch but this stitch is worked on the straight rather than the diagonal. Try different combinations of leaves to create still more patterns.

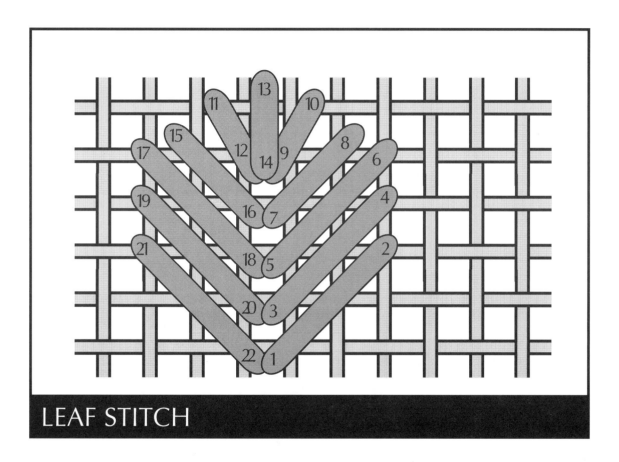

LEAF STITCH

Left-handed instructions for the Leaf Stitch. Left-handers do not need to rotate canvas nor diagram for this stitch. However, if it would be more comfortable to reverse the stitching order, make sure to maintain even padding on the back.

RIBBED WHEELS STITCH

Wheels are durable, decorative and may be used alone as an accent or together for an interesting ground. These stitches are easily rescaled. In reversed wheels the wrapping direction is reversed the ribs are not pronounced at all and the appearance is flatter.

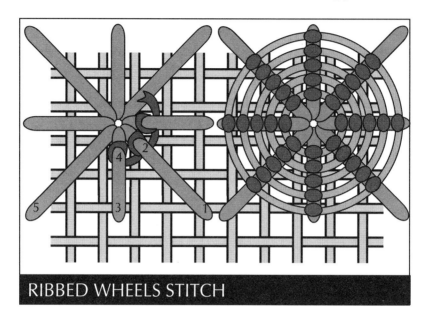

RIBBED WHEELS STITCH

RIBBED WHEELS REVERSE STITCH

Because the wrapping direction is reversed the ribs are not pronounced at all and the appearance is flatter.

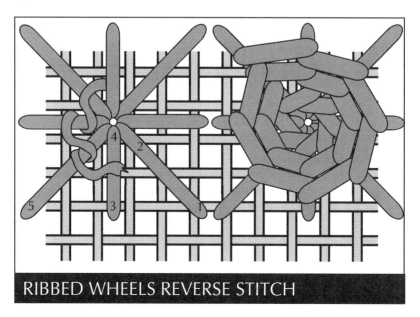

RIBBED WHEELS REVERSE STITCH

Left-handed instructions for Ribbed Wheel Reverse Stitch. Left-handed stitchers will wrap or weave their wheels and spider webs in the reverse directions.

SPIDER WEB STITCH

Spider Web Stitches differ from the Wheels shown because they must always have an odd number of spokes. You simply weave over and under around these spokes, packing in as many threads as you wish to achieve the look you want. We find that you should always add two more rows than you think you need before ending your thread.

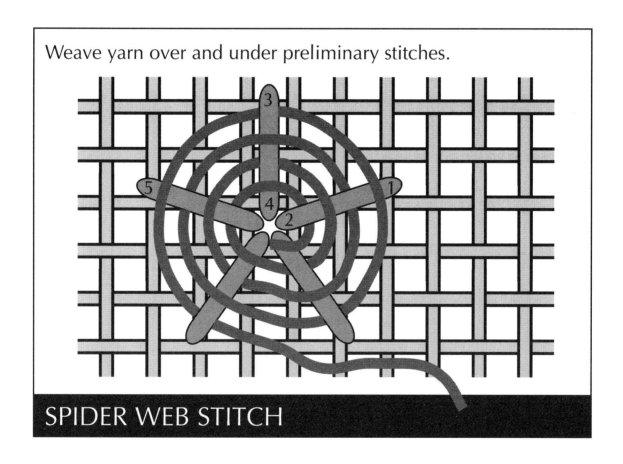

Weave yarn over and under preliminary stitches.

SPIDER WEB STITCH

Left-handed instructions for Ribbed Wheel Reverse Stitch. Left-handed stitchers will wrap or weave their Wheels and Spider Webs in the <u>reverse direction.</u>

TURKEY WORK STITCH

Wait until all the other stitches on your canvas are done before you work this stitch so that your needle won't get caught in the loops while you work the other stitches. The most important thing to remember about this stitch is that you begin and end on top of the canvas. It is the only exception to the numbering system in this book. Enter the center of the stitch from number "1" which is on top of the canvas, and loop over to number "2" which is the end of the stitch. This step is pulled tight. You then leave a loop of whatever length you desire and proceed to the next 2 canvas threads to the right or to the left. You may progress in either direction with this stitch which makes it easy to fill your area without turning your canvas but you will always work from bottom to top. Skip one canvas thread between rows. Some stitchers prefer to scatter the loops while others prefer to have them in neat little rows. If working in a small area, you should crowd the stitches more than usual. Do not cut the loops until you have finished the turkey work area to prevent tangling of the raw ends. When you have finished the Turkey Work Stitch area, cut the loops. Trim the pile to the desired height. Should you want to have the loops remain, you will have to hide your beginning and ending threads. To make loops of equal length, stitch them over a piece of cardboard cut to the desired height.

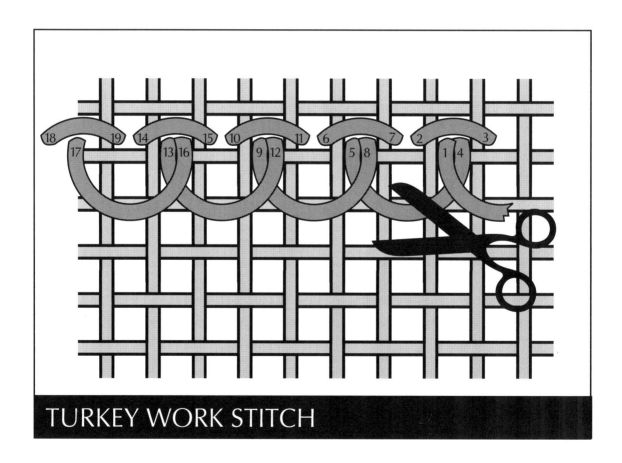

TURKEY WORK STITCH

Left-handed Instructions for Turkey Work Stitch. Rotate the canvas from top to bottom and hold the loops on top, working each row below the one above. Each unit is separate and can be connected left or right, as you wish.

96

Alphabets

Whatever you stitch will likely become an heirloom. For proof you need only to see how much needlework has survived in family collections let alone all the textile collections found in this country's many museums. Therefore, please take pity on those future historians, curators or grandchildren, sign your needlepoint.

Use this basic small alphabet to mark your stitchery. Be sure to include the year. Or, use the larger alphabet on the next page to work a monogram in the center of a sampler or a bargello pillow band as we have done. Someday your great great grandchild will be so happy to know for certain that you were the one who stitched that charming little item. If you really want to earn points with those future curator types, stuff some of the left-over threads inside your finished pillows or behind the dust cover on the back of the framed pieces. If anyone ever needs to patch the item, the threads will be there.

Each square of the chart represents one needlepoint stitch, covering one intersection of the canvas. We do not recommend rescaling either of these alphabets as alphabet design is a very complicated art. If you need a taller or wider alphabet, look through the counted thread books at your local needlework store or library.

Use any kind of graph paper to map out the combination of letters you plan to use. Count the squares used for both letters and spaces. Divide the sum by the canvas mesh size in order to find the size of your stitched monogram or saying.

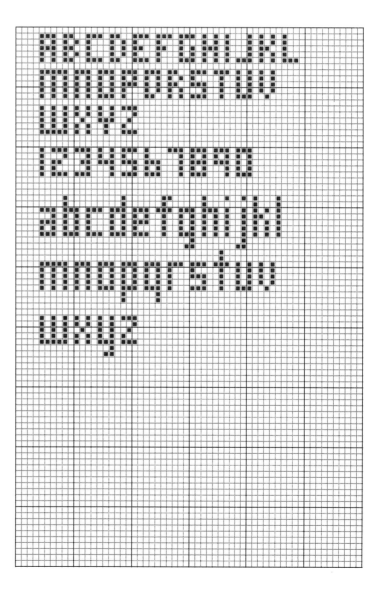

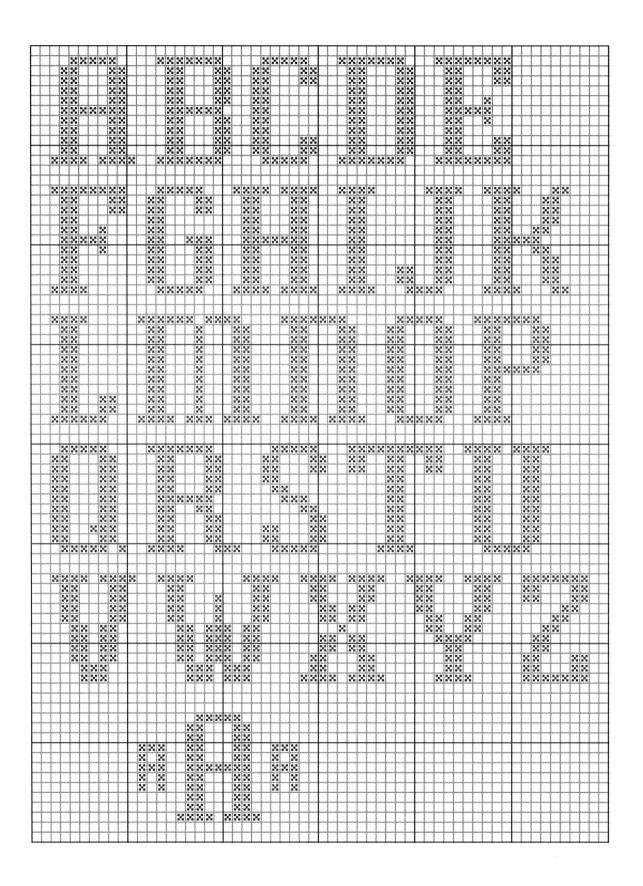

CHAPTER FOUR

THE SAMPLER PROJECTS

It's time to use all those stitches! This chapter contains four projects which contain many of these stitches.

The first project is the Pansy Sampler which features a counted pansy design in the center as well as a border of eight stitches. Refer to the color photo in the book. This is the easiest of the needlepoint projects. The chief lesson for you is this: You can use many of the counted thread chart books at your local needlework shop to find designs you can needlepoint. Use these designs in combination with some of the stitches in this book and create your very own unique needlepoint project.

The second sampler project uses seventeen stitches in the design, which is worked in five shades of dusty blue. The horizontal stripe pattern is photographed in the book. You will notice the horizontal nature of the stripes will force you to compensate each stitch or surround it with tent stitches. We did the basic design but when you stitch this sampler it becomes your own. Please feel free to make changes as you wish. If you choose to use all tent stitches instead of compensation stitches, that is perfectly all right with us. We're very easy to get along with! Whatever you do will help you develop your skills as a needlepoint artist. Enjoy!

The most advanced project is the rectangular sampler photographed in the book. It is worked in the same five shades of blue which are often combined in interesting ways. In order to center elements of the design, there are many compensated areas in the project. However, we want you to enjoy your needlepoint so feel free to make changes. We promise not to look over your shoulder.

The final project in this chapter is a brief introduction to Bargello or Florentine Stitchery. The instructions will be for a strip of needlepoint used to make the pillow band also photographed in the book. Use the larger alphabet on page 98 and any graph paper to plan your monogram for the center area of your Bargello Pillow Band. Divide the number of stitches by the size of the canvas for the size of the letters.

Make one or all of these projects for the sheer joy of it.

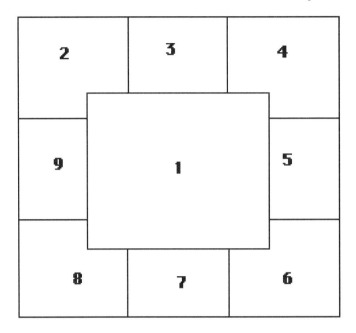

Pansy Centered Sampler
Materials Needed:

16" x 16" Zweigart® White Mono # 12 Canvas
1/4 Pound White Paterna Persian
2-62" strands Bright Yellow Paterna Persian (for flower)
2-62" strands Lavender (for flower)
2-62" strands Dark Burgundy Paterna Persian (for flower)
3-62" strands Dark Green Paterna Persian (for flower)
4-62" strands Medium Green Paterna Persian (for flower)
1 10meter reel Kreinik 1/8 inch Ribbon, Gold
Nepo™ Needlepoint Marking Pen
2 sets of Stretcher Bars 16" each (to use as a working frame)
Staple Gun
Size 20 Tapestry Needle

Marking Your Canvas

Find the center of your canvas by folding in two directions and marking the intersection of the two folds. The center area with the counted pansy design is 54 stitches by 54 stitches. Count out from center 27 threads of canvas in each direction. Mark the border of the center pansy area. It will be a square that is 54 threads by 54 threads or roughly four and one-half inches square. Count out 42 threads from each of these secondary lines to find the outer edge of your pillow. This outer line will mark the perimeter of your stitching area. It will be approximately twelve inches by twelve inches. You should have at least two inches of blank canvas all around the stitching area. Do not remove this canvas as you will need it for blocking and finishing your project.

Count in 48 threads from each corner and mark your canvas. Draw a line from that mark straight up, down or across that thread to the nearest border of the center area. See the diagram. Your canvas should look something like the chart on the preceding page. If so, you will have a center area in which to count your pansy chart. You will have a border composed of 8 areas for your stitches.

Staple your prepared canvas to the frame.

Stitch all the outlines in Kreinik 1/8 inch Ribbon, gold.

All the stitches are to be found in Chapter Three. Note that the Pansy is area No. 1 on the chart. The pansy chart follows on page 102. The other areas are in numerical order clockwise around the perimeter.

2. Diagonal Mosaic Stitch - page 45 - Use 2 ply persian yarn.

3. Scotch Stitch - page 52 - Use 2 ply persian yarn.

4. Milanese Stitch - page 50 - Use 2 ply persian yarn.

5. Gobelin Droit Stitch - page 40 - Use 3 ply persian yarn, work vertically.

6. Jacquard Stitch - page 48- Use 2 ply persian yarn.

7. Double Brick Variation - page 35 - Use 2 ply persian yarn.

8. Double Straight Cross - page 56 - Use 2 ply persian yarn.

9. Gobelin Slanted Stitch over three threads alternating with Continental Tent Stitch. Pages 29 and 47. Use two ply persian yarn for both stitches.

When finished, remove from frame, clean and block if needed. Take it to your needlework shop for finishing as a boxed pillow.

Pansy Chart for Center of Sampler One

Each square of the chart represents one stitch of your needlepoint canvas. Use two ply persian yarn and work this whole area in basketweave or continental tent stitches. Be sure to sign your project in the lower right corner. Use either of the alphabets in this book. Pages 97 and 98.

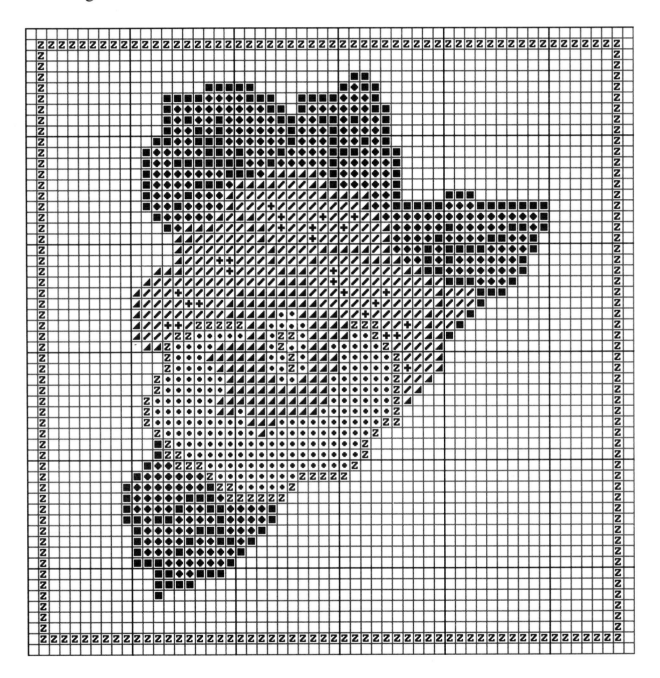

Number	Symbol	Color	Number	Symbol	Color
1	◤	Dark Purple	4	╱	Light Purple
2	■	Dark Green	5	+	Medium
3	⬢	Medium Green	6	Z	Gold
			7	•	Yellow

102

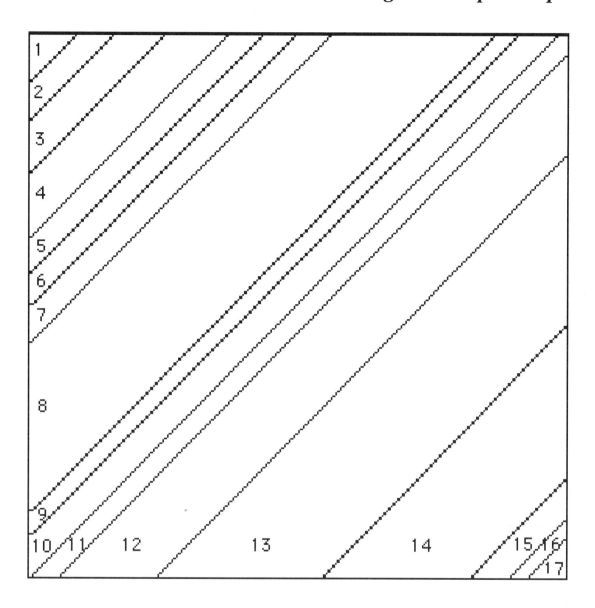

Diagonal Stripe Sampler
Materials Needed:

18" x 18" Zweigart® White Mono Canvas # 13
18 - 62" strands each of 5 shades of Blue Paterna Persian Yarn
2 sets of stretcher bars 18 " each (to use as working frame)
Nepo™Needlepoint Marking Pen
Staple Gun
Size 20 Tapestry Needle

This diagonally striped sampler has a finished size of approximately 14" x 14". Follow the numbers around the edges of the chart on the preceding page. We will tell you the width of each band of stitches and which shade of blue was used. The lightest shade will be Blue No. One and the darkest shade will be Blue No. Five, with Two, Three and Four signifying progressively darker shades of blue.

Begin by marking a 14" square in the center of your canvas. Be sure to allow a border of blank canvas all the way around the perimeter of this marked area. The unworked area must be left on your canvas to be used later for blocking and finishing.

To facilitate marking your canvas, we have listed the seventeen stitch areas of your canvas. The first number listed for each area refers to the thread width of that particular stripe on your canvas. Begin at the upper left, count to the right that many threads and make a mark with your Nepo™ marking pen. Continue to mark across the top of the canvas and then proceed to count down the right side and mark the balance of the stripes. Now, go back to the first mark and carefully mark a diagonal line from upper right to lower left on your canvas. If the first thread intersection is topped by a vertical thread, make sure that each intersection is topped by a vertical thread. Of course, the same applies if the marked intersection is topped by a horizontal thread. Continue to mark each of the diagonal lines on your canvas. When finished, staple your canvas to the stretcher bar frame. You are ready to go to your corner and come out stitching!

1. 18 threads - Diagonal Plaited Stitch. Use 2 ply persian, Blue No. Two and Blue No. four on alternate rows following the chart. Page 44.

2. 26 threads - Diagonal Leaf Stitch Filled with Basketweave at edges. Use Blue No. One for Leaf Stitches and Blue No. Three for fill-in Basketweave Stitches. Page 90.

3. 21 threads - Milanese Stitch worked over first twenty threads using Blue. No. 4. Work one row of chain stitch over the twenty-first row, using Blue No. Five. Page 50.

4. 22 threads - Gobelin Droit Variation Stitch worked with Blue No. 2. The long stitches cover 8 threads of canvas and the shorter stitches cover two threads. Work two long stitches and then two short stitches, centered beside the longer stitches. Repeat across the row. Page 40 but over 8 threads.

5. 4 threads - Diagonal Buttonhole Stitch worked with Blue No. One exactly as shown on chart. Page 89.

6. 6 threads - Gobelin Droit Stitch worked horizontally along the diagonal line over three threads, using Blue No. Two. Work a second row of this stitch, using the same color but turning the stitches so they run in a vertical direction. Page 40.

7. <u>4 threads</u> - Diagonal Buttonhole Stitch worked with Blue No. One, exactly as shown on chart on page 89, BUT <u>rotate the chart 180 degrees.</u> Now you know how those left-handers feel if you are one of those right-handers!

8. <u>40 threads</u> - Hungarian Ground Stitch shown on page 41. Work the zig-zag stitches in Blue No. Two and fill in with Blue No. Three.

9. <u>8 threads</u> - Gobelin Droit Stitch worked horizontally over two threads, using Blue No. Four. Page 47. Now work Diamond Eyelet Stitches over four threads using Blue No. Five. Page 91. Repeat Gobelin Droit horizontally over two threads, using Blue No. Four.

10. <u>6 threads</u> - Diagonal Stitch shown on page 46 as a variation of Scotch Stitch. The Diagonal Stitches are worked in Blue No. Four. Fill in the corners with Blue No. One, using the Basketweave Stitch. Pages 21 - 27.

11. <u>8 threads</u> - Repeat the directions for Number 9.

12. <u>34 threads</u> - Darning Stitch worked vertically, using Blue No. Two. Page 36.

13. <u>34 threads</u> - Use Blue No. Three to work Gobelin Droit Stitch over 3 threads on the diagonal. Switch to Blue No. Five and work Gobelin Droit Stitch vertically over four threads along the same diagonal, abutting the first row. The center area of this section is worked in Blue No. Three. Use the Double Brick Variation Stitch. Page 35. Work it horizontally. Repeat the vertical Gobelin Droit Stitch over four threads in Blue No. Five and then finish this section by repeating the horizontal Gobelin Droit Stitch over three threads on the diagonal.

14. <u>16 threads</u> - Work three repeats of Smyrna Cross Stitches on either edge of this diagonal band. Fill in the middle of the band with vertical Gobelin Droit Stitches worked on the diagonal stripe. Use Blue No. One for all stitches. Page 71.

15. <u>26 threads</u> - Use Blue No. Two for the Victorian Step Stitch. Page 42.

16. <u>4 threads</u> - Use Blue No. Five for the Rococco Stitch shown on page 79.

17.   <u>24 threads or whatever threads remain</u> - Basketweave Stitch as shown on pages 21 - 27. Use Blue No. Four to sign your work using the alphabets on pages 97 and 98. We used three initials from the first alphabet. Work the background of this area in Blue No. Three.

Remove completed needlepoint from frame and prepare for finishing by cleaning and blocking as needed.

Our shop finisher made a non-welted pillow and then trimmed it with a purchased cord. The cord contains all the colors of the backing fabric we chose. We like the added tough of the multi-colored tassels in the upper right corner. These were purchased to match the cording but could easily be made following our directions in the finishing chapter at the end of this book.

Horizontal Stripe Sampler for Advanced Stitchers

Horizontal Stripe Sampler
Materials Needed

16" x 18" Zweigart® White Mono Canvas # 13
18 62" strands each of five shades of Blue Paterna Persian Yarn
1 set of 16" and 1 set of 18" stretcher bars (to use as a working frame)
Nepo™ Needlepoint Marking Pen
Staple Gun
Size 20 Tapestry Needle

107

Mark Your Canvas

Our canvas is 11 1/2" high and 13 1/2" wide.. Begin by using your Nepo™ pen to mark the top and left sides of your canvas to those measurements. You will next mark all the horizontal lines of the project as follows:

Section 1 - Skip 2 threads from the top and make a line across the width of the canvas.

Section 2 - Skip 5 blank threads and mark the 6th across the width of the canvas.

Section 3 - Skip 3 blank threads and mark the 4th across the width of the canvas.

Section 4 - Skip 7 blank threads and mark the 8th across the width of the canvas.

Section 5 - Skip 2 blank threads and mark the 3rd across the width of the canvas.

Section 6 - Skip 23 blank threads and mark the 24th across the width of the canvas.

Section 7 - Skip 2 blank threads and mark the 3rd across the width of the canvas.

Section 8 - Skip 7 blank threads and mark the 8th across the width of the canvas.

Section 9 - Skip 2 blank threads and mark the 3rd across the width of the canvas.

Section 10 - Skip 11 blank threads and mark the 3rd across the width of the canvas.

Section 11 - Skip 2 blank threads and mark the 3rd across the width of the canvas.

Section 12 - Skip 21 blank threads and mark the 3rd across the width of the canvas.

Section 13 - Skip 2 blank threads and mark the 3rd across the width of the canvas.

Section 14 - Skip 13 blank threads and mark the 3rd across the width of the canvas.

Section 15 - Skip Skip 2 blank threads and mark the 3rd across the width of the canvas.

Section 16 - Skip 11 blank threads and mark the 3rd across the width of the canvas.

Section 17 - Skip Skip 2 blank threads and mark the 3rd across the width of the canvas.

Now count 58 threads across from the left and mark this line. Skip one thread and mark the next line. These three stitches will be the center of your project. Compensation stitches will be worked over these center three threads in the Waffle Stitch row and in the Oblong Cross Stitch row. Continue counting 58 threads to the right and mark the right hand edge of your canvas.

Staple your canvas to your stretcher bar frame. You are all set to begin stitching.

The first stitch will cover the top edge line and the two skipped threads of canvas. The second line will be the top thread of the second stitch. Thus, each line will become part of the next stitch until you have reached section 17 which will also include the bottom line of the project.

<u>Stitching Instructions</u>

We have told you the width of each band of stitches and which shade of blue was used. The lightest shade will be Blue No. One and the darkest shade will be Blue No. Four, with Two and Three signifying progressively darker shades of blue. Use two strands throughout the Sampler except in Sections 10 and 12, as noted.

Section 1 - <u>3 Threads</u> - Work Montenegrin Stitch in Blue No. Four over three threads. Page 64.

Section 2 - <u>6 Threads</u> - Work Four Color Herringbone Stitch using all four shades, beginning with Blue No. Four. Page 60.

Section 3 - <u>3 Threads</u> - Repeat Montenegrin Stitch in Blue No. Four over three threads. Page 64.

Section 4 - <u>4Threads</u> - Shell Stitch worked in Blue No. Two over four horizontal threads of the canvas. Use Blue No.Three for the Loop Filling Stitch. Page 77
.

Section 5 - <u>3 Threads</u> - Repeat Montenegrin Stitch in Blue No. Four over three threads. Page 64.

Section 6 - <u>24 Threads</u> - Count twenty-four threads from the left edge of this strip. Divide into nine equal squares of eight threads by eight threads. Refer to photo. Work the William and Mary or Rice Stitch in the four corner segments, using Blue No. Two. Work a Spider Web Stitch in the center square with Blue No.Two. Fill in the remaining small squares with Diamond Eyelet Stitch, using Blue No Three. Skip thirteen threads and repeat this section. Skip another thirteen threads and repeat. Continue across row. You will have five of these square areas separated by four vertical areas, each thirteen threads wide. Pages 69, 95, and 91.

In each of the two outer unworked areas, we worked Tvistom Stitch vertically, using Blue. No. Two. We used Blue No. Four to work in the date vertically over a three stitch wide band in the left area. We worked a monogram into a three stitch wide band included in the right outer area. Page 63

In the two remaining areas we worked three rows of Loop Stitch. Page 76.

Section 7 - 3 Threads - Repeat Montenegrin Stitch in Blue No. Four over three threads. Page 64.

Section 8 - 18 Threads - Use Blue No. One to work Stepped Sheaf Stitch over the middle twelve horizontal threads. Fill in the larger remaining areas with Raised Cross Stitch over six horizontal threads and fill in the smaller unworked areas with Scotch Stitches over 3 horizontal and vertical threads. Page 81.

Section 9 - 3 Threads - Repeat Montenegrin Stitch in Blue No. Four over three threads. Page 64.

Section 10 - 8 Threads - Use Blue No. One to work Chain Stitch across row between the first two horizontal threads. Use one strand of Blue No. Four to place three rows of padding all the way across the canvas from left to right and return. These threads will be held in place by Buttonhole Bar Stitch worked in Blue No. Two, using one ply. Page 88.

Section 11 - 3 Threads - Repeat Montenegrin Stitch in Blue No. Four over three threads. Page 64.

Section 12 - 12 Threads - Work five Giant Rococco Stitches as shown on page 80. Use Blue No. Two, working in one ply. Fill remaining areas of band with the Web Stitch. Page 83. Use Blue. No. Three.

Section 13 - 3 Threads - Repeat Montenegrin Stitch in Blue No. Four over three threads. Page 64.

Section 14 - 18 Threads - Work three rows of Oblong Cross Stitch over seven horizontal threads of canvas, using Blue No. One. Work the tie downs in the same color

110

in rows one and three but use Blue No. Three, alternating with Blue No. One for the tie-downs in the center row. Page 65. Use Blue No. Four to work small Cross Stitches between rows 1 and 2 and rows 2 and 3 in the open spaces left by the Oblong Cross Stitches. Page 55. Use the same Blue No. Four to work French Knots in the remaining open spaces at the top and bottom of this area.

Section 15 - 3 Threads - Repeat Montenegrin Stitch in Blue No. Four over three threads. Page 64.

Section 16 - 14 Threads - Work two rows of Waffle Stitch over 7 horizontal threads. Use Blue No. One and Blue No. Three, alternating the colors in a checkerboard fashion. In the photo you will see that we also alternated the final tie-down color in each square.

Section 17 - 3 Threads - Repeat Montenegrin Stitch in Blue No. Four over three threads. Page 64.

Section 18 - 12 Threads - Work Herringbone Gone Wrong Stitch in Blue. No. three. Page 61.

Section 19 - 3 Threads - Repeat Montenegrin Stitch in Blue No. Four over three threads. Page 64.

Bargello Band for Double Bow Pillow

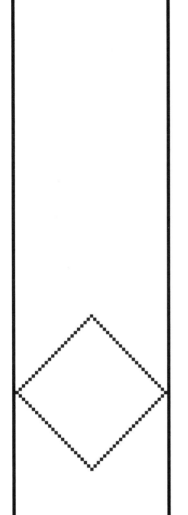

Bargello Band
Materials Needed:

25" x 8" Zweigart Brown Bargello Canvas #13
15 - Strands 62" long of each of Four shades of
    Paterna Persian Yarn, Dusty Blue
10" Wide Roller Bar Frame
Tape of Staple Gun (to attach canvas to frame.)
Nepo™ Marking Pen
Size 20 Tapestry Needle

Use your pen to mark an area four inches wide by twenty-one inches, lengthwise along your canvas. Be sure the length of the canvas is parallel to the selvage edge of the canvas. Find the center of this marked strip and carefully mark a diagonal square area for your monogram, as shown in the accompanying chart.

Use the lightest blue for the background of the central area and work your monogram with the darkest blue. Use two ply for the Basketweave and Continental Tent Stitches used in this area. Pages 20 to 27 in the book. Refer to the larger alphabet. Page 98.

See the chart for the Basic Florentine Stitch. Page 38. Working from dark to light, repeat this pattern in both directions from the central monogram area. Use three ply of Paterna Persian Yarn for the Florentine Stitch.

When you have finished stitching, remove from frame, clean and block. Refer to the finishing chapter for complete instructions on making this band and the accompanying "bow" pillows as shown on our cover.

This project, in particular, is so quick to stitch and to finish, that it is ideal for giving your home a quick decorating "pick me up." Great gift too!

CHAPTER FIVE

PROJECTS FROM START TO FINISH

Your local needlework store has many needlepoint projects ready and waiting for you. Occasionally you will want to design your own. We could write a whole book on the subject but we will briefly try to give you the basics of designing on canvas.

There are thousands of charts available that you can use as is or in combination. If you can draw, make a black and white "cartoon" of your intended design. Place the cartoon under your canvas and trace off the design elements with a Nepo or similar "safe" pen. You can have any existing picture enlarged or shrunk at your photo-copy store to be traced in the same way. Look at greeting cards, scarves, wrapping paper and coloring books for ideas. **Warning**: You may only copy designs for your own use. To sell designs made from copywrited sources is against the law.

If you choose to paint your canvas, we suggest you use a good quality acrylic paint such as Liquitex™ or Hyplar™. Buy the artists tubes and thin to the consistency of thick cream. If you buy a small set of colors, you can mix anything you desire. As you paint, make sure you cover the threads of the canvas. Do not clog the holes. Allow the canvas to dry thoroughly before stitching. Even though acrylic paints are "colorfast," it is always wise to test them. When dry, rub the painted area with a dampened white towel. If the color lifts, you have two options. Either rinse the canvas under running cold water until the water runs clear or, seal the entire canvas with a clear polymer varnish such as Krylon™. If you choose the first method, you will have to block the canvas before stitching. If you choose the second method, you will have to blow on the canvas to make sure the holes remain open.

Commercial canvas is normally sold in 40 or 54 inch widths. If you plan a project to be wider than that, it must be stitched on 2 or more pieces of canvas. Once stitched, these pieces are joined along a seam or join line. Canvases this large are rarely available ready-made. Most shops have artists who will be glad to work with you.

Or, you can do this yourself by following our instructions.

It is important to thoroughly plan your project on paper before transferring the design to canvas. When your line drawing is completed to your satisfaction, measure it and mark it where it will have to be separated. Draw an additional pencil line on either side of the join line. The pencil lines should be 1 inch from the join line. See the illustration.

You are now ready to put your design on canvas.

Our sample design is 40 inches by 70 inches and will be worked on 54 inch wide canvas. The pieces will be placed on the canvas as illustrated. Be sure to maintain your two inch borders all around each piece.

Separate the canvases and stitch according to the next illustration.

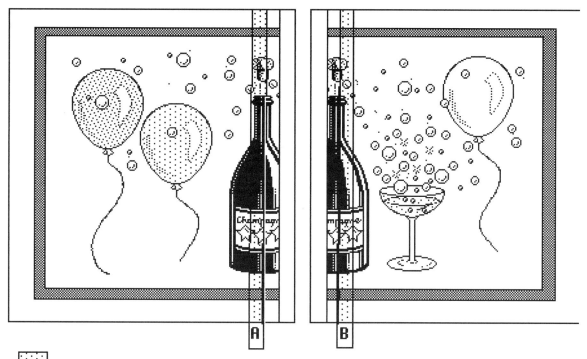

The area to be joined – DO NOT STITCH UNTIL PIECES HAVE BEEN BLOCKED AND ARE READY TO BE JOINED.

Stitch both pieces of canvas up to the shaded join line. Block in the usual manner and place the join areas side by side on a large table. If you are right-handed, place join area B on top of join are A.

If you are left-handed place join area A on top of join area B. Be sure to match the design areas carefully.

You will be stitching through both shaded areas A and B as though they are one canvas. The only way to do this is to poke stitch. If you use a sewing motion the two pieces of canvas are too likely to slip and your join will not be right.

DO NOT WORRY ABOUT THE EXCESS THREADS ON TOP OF YOUR CANVAS. When the canvas has been joined, turn it over to the wrong side. Unravel the vertical threads from the excess canvas. Take a pair of very sharp pointed scissors and VERY CAREFULLY cut away the horizontal threads right up to the join line so they you see only the faintest little bit of canvas if any. Turn the canvas to the right side and again unravel the vertical threads and cut the horizontal threads right up to the join. Do not cut your needlepoint. Find a strong friend to help you with the next step. Give one end of the canvas to your friend. You hold the other end. Now tug! Any remaining little cut ends of canvas threads will disappear into the body of the needlepoint.

115

There are other ways to join canvas, most of them easier and faster than this method. However, no other join will be practically invisible nor will it be as long-wearing as the body of your needlepoint project. This join satisfies both requirements.

AN IMPORTANT HINT! Whatever method you use to design your canvas, be sure to save the outline for use as a guide when blocking and finishing your project.

FINISHING

If you are adding any sort of embellishments to your canvas wait until the piece is cleaned and blocked.

Cleaning Your Canvas

No matter how careful you have been while stitching, your needlepoint might need cleaning before finishing.. Unless you are absolutely certain that your dry cleaner is experienced and skilled at cleaning needlepoint, you are better off to do it yourself. There is a commercial cleaner on the market named Stitch Clean™. It is a neutral PH product and easy to use. Simply spray the cleaner on any soiled areas and gently blot with a clean sponge until the soil is gone. If this product is not available, use the suds <u>only</u> from a gentle solution of Ivory Snow or some similar product. Do not use any liquid detergents. Make sure you remove all soapy residue carefully. We do not recommend any other commercial products as most have not been tested over a long enough time period. The textile department of your local art museum should be able to offer suggestions to you. If you have stitched with silk and find it needs cleaning, take it to a cleaner who has a reputation for cleaning fine silk garments. Make him promise to use fresh cleaning fluid. Be warned that most silk flosses are not color fast. If you are not certain about <u>any</u> of the fibers you have used, test samples of each fiber individually by wetting it tosee if the colors run. If the colors are not fast, you will want to dry block and only spot clean those areas stitched in color-fast fibers.

Preparing Your Canvas

Make certain that you have not skipped any stitches. It is easier to do this while you work by holding your piece up to the light. If you have missed any stitches, you should see them. However, no matter how careful you are, the "Unstitch Gremlin" will come along and remove a few stitches in the middle of the night. Fight back! When you have completed your needlepoint, have another stitcher look over your piece for you. Before proceeding, make sure all thread ends have been secured and clipped close to the back of your canvas. If you do not secure all thread ends carefully, you will be amazed at how many "missed" stitches you will find when your piece has been finished or framed. If you did not remove the selvage edge before stitching, do it now. The extra tight weave of the selvage will forever hold the stitches on that edge of the canvas differently from the other edge.

Blocking Your Canvas

Even if you have worked your needlepoint on a frame, blocking is important to improve the final appearance of your project. Blocking evens the stitches and restores the canvas to its original shape. You can use a commercial blocking board or T-pins and your ironing board. The board should be larger than the needlepoint which needs to be blocked. With either device you will place the needlepoint face down if stitched with tent stitches and face up if stitched with other decorative type stitches.

For traditional blocking methods, you will need a plant mister bottle, a waterproof pen, a sheet of white paper, galvanized nails, T-pins, rust proof staples, and a piece of cork board covered in fabric or Contact™ paper. You can use a board other than cork as long as it is soft enough to readily take tacks or T-pins. You can use an item called a Four-Square Blocker manufactured by Marie Products. It comes with its own supply of galvanized nails and has painted lines and circles on the board which serve as guides to blocking. It is available from your local needlework shop. This device has pre-drilled holes in straight lines all over the surface so that you can straighten your canvas easily by lining up the nail-holes along a thread of the canvas just outside the stitched area. As you place the nails in the holes, you can exert some tension to help in stretching the canvas. If you did not make a template before stitching, use the pen to draw the shape of your finished project on the paper. Place the template in the center of your blocking board. If you have a cartoon or template, use this in the same manner.

Spray the needlepoint piece lightly. Stretch and pin or nail to the contours you have drawn on the paper. If you are not certain all the fibers are color-fast, do not wet your canvas at all. Using a steam iron, gently steam but do not press your needlepoint. Protect your work with a pressing cloth. Place the board flat on the floor or table top. Wet or dry, allow the canvas to rest in this position for at least 48 hours while the canvas threads return to their original state. If your canvas is seriously out of alignment, you may need to repeat the process.

Do not rush the blocking process. Consider how many hours you have already invested in your stitching!

If the piece should start to run, remove it immediately from the blocking board and hold under cold running water until all excess dye is removed and the water runs clean. Do not allow it to dry until you are satisfied with its appearance.

Embellishing Your Canvas

When you have successfully cleaned and blocked your needlepoint, it is time to add any surface embellishments that you have chosen. Add some glitz to your design with sew-on rhinestones and metal charms. Refer to the color pictures in this book. These add-ons are called "Charming Glitters" and are available at local needlework and craft stores by Kappie Originals Ltd. Try adding beads, sew-on ribbon roses, or little wooden miniatures to your needlepoint. Visit hobby, miniature and sewing stores for all sorts of fun embellishments you can use to make your needlepoint uniquely yours. Avoid studs because the prongs would tear the fibers and canvas threads of your project. If you must use studs, use a hand stud-setter so that you can place the prongs between the canvas threads. It would be best to do this before stitching.

Finishing Techniques Such as Stitching, Sewing, and Framing

Stitchery projects such as eyeglass cases, bell pulls, and rugs, are within the ability of every needlepointer to finish. We have included directions for finishing these items in this book. Those of you who sew will also find directions for making pillows. We have also included instructions for preparing your project for framing.

We want to share some of our thoughts about finishing skills. Consider that you have spent money for your supplies and a great many hours working on your needlepoint. It would be a shame to do anything to damage your project because you lack the skills or equipment to properly finish the item in question. Certain finished items such as most purses and belts, pillows, and upholstered pieces are best left to professionals unless you yourself own the proper equipment. If you are a skilled machine sewer and understand the principles of putting together clothing or slipcovers you will have no trouble putting together any of the needlepoint projects in this book. If you are not skilled in these areas, please do not attempt to learn on a project that you have just spent the last six months to create. The shop where you purchase your supplies most certainly will have a finisher to complete your item.

Hand Finishing - No Machine Needed

The first stitch diagramed in the stitch section called cross stitches is the Binding Stitch. With this one stitch you can finish a great many needlepoint items yourself, whether stitched on interlocked, mono or plastic canvas.We usually add one ply to the yarn used for finishing to make sure that we completely cover all the raw canvas. This extra padding adds to the wearability of the item.

Unstitched plastic canvas makes an excellent stiffener for needlepoint projects. It is chemically inert and will not harm your needlepoint over the years. Cut it 1/8 inch shorter in all directions than your finished project. Adding such stiffening is a matter of personal preference.

At times it is necessary to join two worked pieces of needlepoint together, such as the front and back of a purse or a two-sided key tag. Do not work the binding stitch on either of these pieces until they are to be joined. The binding stitch then becomes your Joining Stitch. Refer to the Binding Stitch Instructions on Page 54 for complete information.

TRIMS AND TASSELS

Twisted Cord

Twisted cord is a useful trim the hand finisher can use on a number of needlepoint projects. It is easier to make when done by two people. Measure the outside of your project and multiply by three. This is a good working length for one strand of twisted cord. You will need to determine how many strands you should use, according to the desired thickness of the finished cord. Start out with six strands and do some practice twists.

After cutting the desired number of cord lengths, gather them together and tie each end with a knot. Find the center and tie a knot there as well. Put a pencil between the strands at each end, as illustrated to the right.

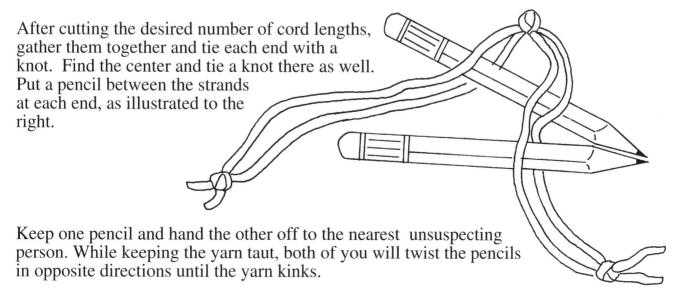

Keep one pencil and hand the other off to the nearest unsuspecting person. While keeping the yarn taut, both of you will twist the pencils in opposite directions until the yarn kinks.

119

Keep the yarn taut while you hook the knotted center section over a finger. Hand your pencil to the same unsuspecting person you convinced to help you. That person now holds both pencils while you make sure that the yarn remains taut. See the accompanying illustration.

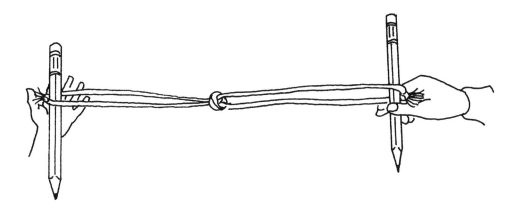

Remove the center knot from your finger. To insure an even twist and a pretty cord, <u>slowly</u> release the tension as the two pieces twist together.

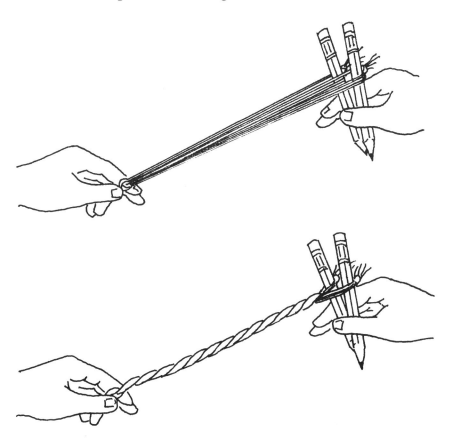

Sew the ends together so that your cord will not untwist. Remove the pencils. Sew the cord in place on the edge of your needlepoint project with small blind stitches.

TASSELS

To make tassels wrap yarn around a piece of cardboard. The length of the cardboard will determine the length of your tassels. The number of wraps will determine the thickness of your tassels. Notice that the loose ends are at the bottom of the cardboard. When you have wrapped enough yarn, tie it all together at the top of the cardboard with a strand of yarn at least 12 inches long. Remove from cardboard. Take another 12 inch strand of yarn and tie it around your tassel, about 3/4 inch from top to form the bead at the top. Cut the loops on the bottom and trim the ends as desired. See the accompanying illustration.

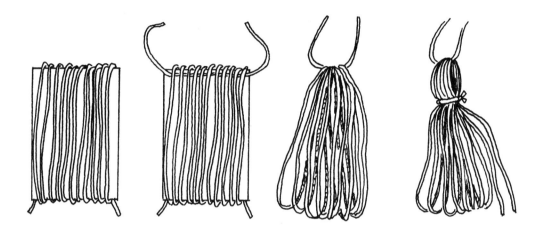

Now that you have a good stitch repertoire and a knowledge of basic finishing techniques, you should be able to fashion an endless variety of needlepoint items for home, family and friends. There are hundreds of projects suitable for needlepoint. We have included many of the most popular items in this book.

PROJECTS

BELL PULLS

Planning and Design

Bell pulls are usually about 36 inches long and 6 inches wide but we have seen old ones in museums that were as long as 72 inches. Consider where you plan to hang your bell pull. Many bell pull designs are available at your local needlework shop. It is wise to order the hardware when you purchase the canvas. Buy bell pull hardware about 1/4 inch wider than the stitched width of your needlepoint. Shop personnel will be glad to assist you in your selection. If you design your own bell pull, use the samplers or bargello patterns in this book. Select your hardware and purchase canvas that is four inches longer than your finished design. Be sure to leave a two inch margin of unworked canvas on each of the four sides of your bell pull. Roll up and save the remaining canvas for the other projects in this book.

Note: To hang properly when finished, the bell pull must be laid out along the straight grain of the canvas. The grain runs in the same direction as the red line at the selvage edge of the canvas. Remove the selvage and tape the raw edges before you begin to stitch.

A bell pull is one of the easiest pieces to finish. It should always be finished by hand. You should have removed the selvage edge of your needlepoint before stitching. If not, remove this edge before blocking. Failure to remove the selvage is the single most important cause of warped and mis-shaped bell pulls.

After blocking your needlepoint, trim the canvas to within one inch of the stitched area. Cut a piece of lining fabric to this same size. Buy enough lining fabric so that you can cut the lining on the straight of the fabric. The straight of the fabric is parallel to the selvage edge. If you don't cut your lining along this grain, the finished bell pull will not hang properly. Fold in the raw edges of the needlepoint along the two long sides, leaving two threads of unworked canvas exposed along both edges. Work the binding stitch over those two exposed canvas threads on both long edges of your bell pull. Do not worry about the top and bottom at this time. Take your lining fabric and fold in the side edges of your lining until it is the same width as your needlepoint. Press the lining at this time. Never press your needlepoint! Thread your needle, attach thread with a knot to one end of side edge of the lining. Use short little blind stitches to attach this lining to the back edge of the binding stitch you have worked along the edges of the needlepoint. (To make little blind stitches, make a tiny overcast stitch to join lining and binding stitch, then run needle under fold of lining about 1/4 inch, come up and repeat across the length of fabric.)

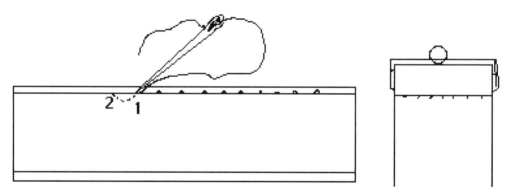

Blind Stitch Illustration (Most of Stitch is Hidden Under Thread - Thus, the Blind Stitch)

When you have finished sewing both sides, you will be ready to make a casing at top and bottom to hold your bell pull hardware. The width of the casing will be determined by the hardware. Once this width is determined, you will fold over each end twice to hide the raw edges. Use the same blind stitch technique to secure the casing. See the illustration above.

To end your thread, do a few overlapping stitches for strength and then break off. Insert the rod and fasten to the hardware. If your hardware has a small ring on one end and large ring on the other, place the small ring at the top for hanging on the wall. The larger ring is for you to pull when you call your butler. We hope he comes faster than ours.

THE BILL MILLAN BELT

Bill is one of our favorite customers. He has made at least 50 belts using this technique which he shared with us. Go to your local discount store and purchase a belt with leather tabs on each end like the Pot of Gold Belt illustrated in this book. If you buy a belt that fits, you will know what size to make your needlepoint. Carefully remove the leather ends from the belt. Leave the buckle installed. Set the tabs aside while you measure a piece of canvas the same size as the body of the belt you just removed. Add two inches to this measurement. Use the four color herringbone pattern or a Bargello pattern or design your own belt. After stitching, block your needlepoint in the usual manner. Bind the long edges with the binding stitch. Use grosgrain ribbon the width of your belt as a lining or use a strip of thin leather, if available. The leather may be glued in place. Use an awl or an ice pick to open the stitching holes of the leather tabs. Sew the tabs in place on your new belt.

CHECKBOOK COVER

Checks and registers come in all sorts of formats so your best bet is to use the cover given to you by the bank as a model. Look at it carefully to see where you will need openings to insert the checks. Add 1/4 inch to all the measurements of your model to allow for the thickness of the stitching and for your binding stitch finish. We are describing the finishing techniques for a standard three by six inch purse-size check book. You will need to plan a design that looks nice on each half of a folded six-inch square of needlepoint. See illustration. Be sure to add two inches of unstitched canvas on all four sides. Your canvas will measure ten inches by ten inches.

 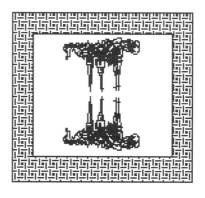

Illustration of Checkbook Cover With Design on Both Halves

Needlepoint fabric is a wonderful choice for a checkbook cover because of its wearability. The finishing should be by hand and is relatively quick to do. After you have blocked your 6 inch square needlepoint, trim to within 1/2 inch of the stitching and fold all the raw edges to the inside. Work the binding stitch around all four edges, mitering the corners as shown in the following illustration.

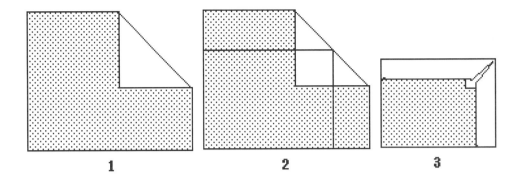

Illustratio

n Showing Proper Method for Mitering Corners

Cut a piece of moire lining fabric about 1/2 inch larger all the way around than your needlepoint. Using the blind stitch, stitch the lining to the binding stitch all the way around. The lining is shown as striped fabric in the illustration. The white area is a second lining that is used to hold your checks and check register in place. The top piece will be cut three inches by seven inches and then folded to two inches by six inches and sewn in place where the heavy lines are on the illustration. The unsewn edge will wear better if it is folded twice to cover the raw edges which are glued with Unique Stitch™ or some other thick white fabric glue. This edge is not attached to the lining but is left open for the insertion of the check register.

For the bottom half, cut a piece of lining fabric six inches wide by three inches high. Fold over the raw edges until it measures two inches high by five inches wide. Attach the right and lower edges to the lining of the checkbook cover with blind stitches. Again, glue the other two edges for strength, as above. These two edges are also not attached to anything, in order to facilitate the insertion of your checks. See the illustration to the right.

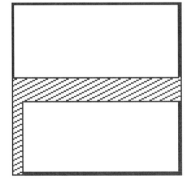

Illustration of Inside of Checkbook Cover

COASTERS

Finished coasters are usually four inches by four inches square. Allow about two inches on all sides for blocking and finishing. To conserve canvas, lay them out in a row about four inches apart and work and block together. See illustration.

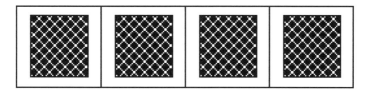

Illustration Showing Layout for One Set of Coasters

After you have blocked your needlepoint, trim each square to within 1/2 inch of the stitching and fold all the raw edges to the inside. Work the binding stitch around all four edges, mitering the corners as shown in the section on finishing bell pulls. Line the coaster with two or three layers of medium weight Pellon™. It would be a nice touch to glue a square of cork to the bottom of your coaster, but this is not necessary as cork may be hard to find in your area. Be sure to allow your coasters to air dry before storing.

EYEGLASS CASE

Finished standard eyeglass cases usually measure three inches by six inches. If you make a case for half glasses, make your case two inches by six inches.

There are two basic ways to make a needlepoint eyeglass case. The first method is to work a single piece of needlepoint six inches square. The other method is to use two pieces of fabric that are each three inches by six inches. (One piece could be simply a sturdy backing fabric, or both pieces could be needlepoint.) In either case, to finish with the binding stitch, simply trim your needlepoint to within 1/2 inch of the stitching on all four sides of each piece. Cut lining fabric to match these trimmed pieces in size. Fold the raw edges to the inside and work the binding stitch all around the four sides, mitering the corners as above. Use the blind stitch again to fasten the lining to each piece of needlepoint. If a one piece needlepoint case, after the lining is sewn in place, you will fold your eyeglass case in half with the lining to the inside and join the bottom and side seams. The joining stitch should be a running stitch going from back to front between the binding stitches. You will leave the top open for inserting your glasses. If a two piece case, after front and back have been lined, put them together with the lining inside and join the 2 long sides and the bottom as illustrated to the right.

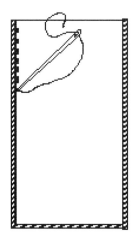

Illustration of Running Stitch

KEY TAGS

Work an eyelet stitch into the top corner of the front and back for your chain or key ring. Make sure the eyelets will line up when the 2 pieces are joined with the raw edges together. See illustration which shows the 2 insides of the key tag . Stitch front and back to the desired size and fold over all four edges of each piece so that only one canvas thread is on the fold. Miter all the corners and join the two sides together with the binding stitch. One thread from either side of the key tag will make the two threads normally used for the binding stitch. Insert a chain or ring through the eyelets and add your keys.

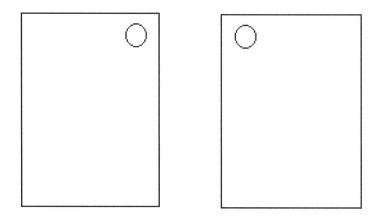

Illustration Showing Placement of Hole in Key Tags

MAGNETS

Trim and finish as you would for a coaster. Line with a piece of felt which is sewn to the binding stitch on the back. Glue a large magnet to the felt. Magnets are available at most craft stores.

PAPERBACK BOOK COVER

Block your three pieces of needlepoint, the front, the spine and the back. Trim to within 1/2 inch of your stitching. Join the front to the front edge of the spine with the binding stitch. Join the back to the back edge of the spine with the binding stitch. Work the binding stitch around the outside edge of your book cover. Your lining fabric must be large enough to fold back as a flap to hold the front and back book covers in place. Therefore, you will measure your joined pieces of needlepoint from the front edge across the front, the spine and the back to the back open edge. Add seven inches to this measurement. The height of your lining will the height of your bound needlepoint book cover plus one inch. Fold in 1/2 inch of lining at either side and press in place. Then fold in 3 inches on either end and press again. See illustration.

Illustration Showing Outside and Inside of Book Cover
Heavy line represents binding stitch on front. Light line represents folded lining inside.

Join the lining to the needlepoint with a blind stitch. If you wish to have a book mark, insert a ribbon between the lining and the needlepoint at the top edge of the spine.

FOLD-OVER CLUTCH PURSE OR SCISSORS CASE

Determine the height and width of your finished purse or scissors case. You will need to stitch a piece of canvas that is 3 times the finished height by the chosen width. Make a paper model of this. Fold it as it will be used to see the direction your design must go on each section. To make a scissors case, measure the length and width of your favorite pair of embroidery scissors. Add 1/4 inch to each of these measurements and proceed as above. When you have determined the amount of canvas needed for your purse or scissors case, be sure to add two inches all the way around each piece for blocking and finishing. After stitching, block and trim to within 1/2 inch of the stitching and cut a piece of lining fabric to this size. Fold the raw edges to the inside and work the binding stitch around all 4 sides, mitering the corners as you go. Blind stitch the lining to the binding stitch. Fold up the bottom 1/3 of the needlepoint and join the 2 side seams with a whip stitch. Fold down the top edge and use a self-adhesive Velcro™ dot as a purse closure or buy a magnetic purse closure at your local sewing store.

See illustration on following page.

In the illustration, the heavy lines represent the side seams of the purse.They will be joined by sewing through the binding stitch as illustrated in the eyeglass case instructions.

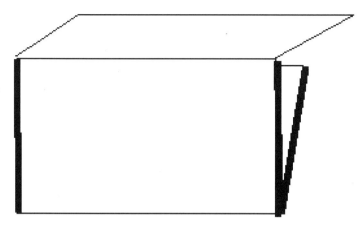

Illustration of Fold-Over Clutch Purse

TISSUE CASE

A tissue case can be easily made using the same method as the purse above. Your needlepoint should be twice the dimensions of the finished size.

You will need to measure the pocket tissue package you normally carry. Double this measurement and add 1/2 inch to the longer measurement to allow for finishing and for the thickness of the tissues. Our finishing technique puts the seam at the center top opening so you must consider this in your design. Again use a paper pattern to assist you in your design.

Block, trim, bind and line as above. To have a seam in the center for extracting tissues, fold your case with the lining to the inside so that the seam will be right across the center of the top of the case. Whip the binding stitch edges together about 1 inch in from either side and then whip the end seam together on one side. You need to leave the other side open for inserting the package of tissues.

Illustration of Tissue Case Layout Before Finishing

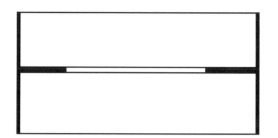

The illustration to the left shows the joined tissue case. The binding stitch is worked over the heavy lines and also around the opening.

PILLOW APPLIQUE

Block your needlepoint canvas, work the binding stitch all the way around, mitering corners as you go and then attach to a ready-made pillow. To attach, simply use the blind stitch technique to catch the underside of the binding stitch to the pillow. A nice touch would be the addition of two handmade tassels to match the binding stitch. One of the lower corners would be a good place for the tassels.

Instead of using the binding stitch, fold under the raw edges of the canvas and sew to the pillow top. Cover the edge with twisted cord and tassels made according to our instructions at the beginning of the chapter.

PILLOW TAB

To Be Inserted In Seam of Pre-finished Pillow

Measure the pillow you plan to embellish with your pillow tab. Your finished tab should be as long as the pillow is tall. The width would usually be about 3 to 4 inches, but a very wide tab might be nice too. It depends on the design. The illustration shows a finished pillow tab.

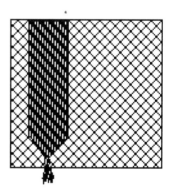

Illustration of Pillow Tab

A pillow tab is finished exactly as the fold-over clutch purse except that the top edge does not need to be sewn. This is the edge that will be inserted into a pre-finished pillow. Purchase a pillow in a coordinating fabric. When you have decided where to place your pillow tab (whether centered or off-centered) simply open the seam at that point and insert the raw edge of your finished pillow tab. Use a blind stitch on either side of the pillow tab to reclose the seam into which you have inserted the pillow tab.

RUG OR WALL HANGING

Before buying or designing your own rug, measure the area in which you are going to use it. If you will be designing your own rug, consider that canvas is normally sold in 40 or 54 inch widths and plan accordingly. If you need to piece your rug, make sure you plan for that before you lay out your design, as the join will have be accounted for on each piece of canvas. See the complete instructions for joining needlepoint canvas at the beginning of this chapter.

Needlepoint is ideal for making rugs because of its strength and wearability. Work your rug in a strong stitch such as basketweave and use a good quality wool. It will last for generations - even if you walk on it.To line or not to line a rug is the big question. We feel that a lining becomes a dirt catcher. The dirt works its way through the rug as it is walked on and becomes trapped by the lining. This trapped dirt rubs against the back of the needlepoint stitches and actually abraids them. If a rug is not lined, it can be flipped over regularly and vacuumed. Rugs used as wall-hangings are often lined for extra body.

After cleaning and blocking, trim the raw edges to within six threads of the needlepoint. Measure off enough rug binding tape to go all the way around the four sides of the rug, plus four inches. You can usually find this tape at an upholstery or sewing store. Since the tape does not show, you can buy any neutral dark or light tone you prefer. Work the binding stitch all the way around the rug and join the rug binding to all four sides. Be sure to miter the corners of the binding tape, as you go. Secure the other edge of the binding to the back of your rug, all the way around. Use tiny overlapping stitches which you catch gently into the back of your needlepoint stitches, making sure that these new stitches do not poke through to the top side of the rug. Use your rug and enjoy it.Vacuum it regularly, both front and back and send it to a good oriental rug cleaner when vacuuming alone won't do.

If you are using your rug for a wall hanging, cut a piece of heavy linen canvas to the size of the blocked and trimmed rug. Work the binding stitch on all four sides. Attach the lining to the binding stitch, being sure to miter all four corners. Leave a small opening on either side of the rug at the top edge. You can insert a rod here for hanging the rug on the wall.Though your rug is hanging on the wall, it should still be vacuumed regularly.

If you want fringe on the ends of your rug, omit the binding stitch from the sides to be fringed. Work turkey tufting there with a 10/2 linen thread, leaving the uncut loops as long as the desired length of the fringe. If you want knotted fringe, add about four inches to the length of the loop. When all the fringe is cut, gather six or eight strands together and tie an overhand knot near the rug edge. Repeat until all the fringe has been knotted. Look at finished oriental or Spanish rugs for ideas.

There are some basic steps that you will take for all machine finished pillows.

We assume that you have good basic sewing skills and have experience in assembling items for your home.

Please refer back to this section.

Materials Needed:

You will need the following for the average size pillow.

Needlepoint, stitched and blocked
1/2 Yard Fabric (Backing and Welting)
1/2 Yard Muslin (Inner pillow)
Polyfil™ Stuffing
Cotton Cord (Measure Perimeter of Finished Pillow Plus Four Inches For Welting)
Tassels and/or Other Trims (If Desired)
Zipper (If Desired)
Matching Thread
Straight Pins
Scissors
Heavy Duty Sewing Machine
Cording Foot*
*zipper foot is adequate if cording foot is not available for your machine

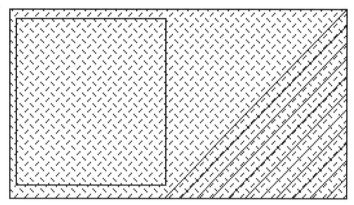

Use half of fabric for backing and the other half to cut into bias strips for welting.

Most any fabric that coordinates with your needlepoint design is suitable. Of course, you will want something as durable as your needlepoint. Try to avoid slippery shiny fabrics such as rayons or fabrics that are too thick to sew on your machine or too thin to handle the stresses involved in upholstery techniques. Velvets, corduroys, and trigger cloth are ideal fabrics.

Trim your needlepoint canvas to within six canvas threads of the stitching. Your machine sewing will be two threads inside the needlepoint stitched area. See Diagram.

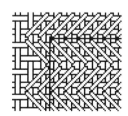

Illustration of Machine Sewing Line

131

This next illustration shows the stitching line in relation to the unstitched area.

The dark line shows that you are actually stitching within the finished needlepoint area The white area of the illustration is the blank canvas. The unsewn area allows for turning the pillow right side out. You will leave an opening like this on all your pillows unless using a zipper. Be sure to clip all corners perpendicular to the seam line or notch them at the corners to prevent puckering.

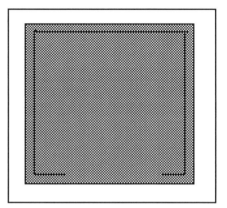

Make your inner pillow first. You should cut muslin large enough to make an inner pillow that is 1 inch larger than your finished needlepoint pillow. Allow 1/2 inch for seams all the way around.   Put right sides together and sew around all four sides, leaving a 6 inch opening on one side for turning. Turn your inner pillow right side out, stuff as firmly as you desire and hand sew the opening closed.

Knife-Edged Pillow Without Welting - Tassel Optional

If you are not going to use welting, you will make your needlepoint pillow exactly as you did your inner pillow. Cut your backing fabric to the size of your trimmed needlepoint canvas. Lay right sides of backing and needlepoint together. Sew around all four sides, being sure to stitch 2 threads into your needlepoint, as shown in the earlier illustration. Leave an opeening along the bottom edge for inserting your inner pillow. If you stitch a smooth curve as you round the corners, your finished pillow will be less likely to have ears. Insert the inner pillow. Hand stitch the opening along the bottom to finish your pillow. If you wish to sew tassels into the corners, see the accompanying diagram.

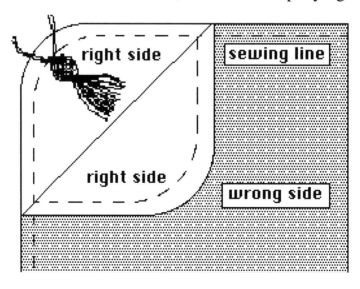

Diagram of Tassel Insertion at Pillow Corner

132

Welting

To make welting, cut your backing fabric on the bias in two inch wide strips. Fold this over the cotton cord (right side out) and sew.Use a cording or zipper foot on your machine. **Note**: Making welting is one of those basic sewing skills which you should know if you are to successfully make a corded needlepoint pillow.

Knife Edged Pillow With Welting

Pin welting in place around the perimeter of your **needlepoint**. Be sure that raw edge is to the outside and that the seam of the welting is right above your sewing line (two threads inside the needlepoint). Sew the welting in place with the welting seam at the bottom of the pillow edge. Complete the pillow in the same manner as the basic knife-edged pillow above. Be sure to sew on the same stitching line as you used for sewing the welting. Turn right side out and insert the inner pillow. Hand finish the closure. If you wish to use a zipper, insert it in a bottom seam according to instructions on the zipper package.

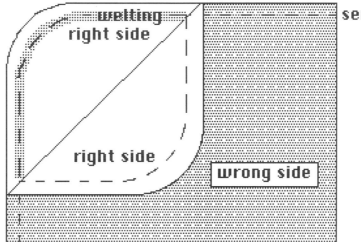

Diagram of Pillow Backing Construction With Welting

Double Bow Pillow for Needlepoint Band

The pillows pictured in the book are 14 inches by 20 inches and the band is 21 inches long and three inches wide. Make two cordless knife edged pillows of fabric to match your project. The top one will be two inches narrower. These pillows should be stuffed loosely. Finish the needlepoint band as you would a bell pull but sew Velcro™ to each end instead of making a casing. Wrap the band around the two pillows, cinching them so that they form a bow.

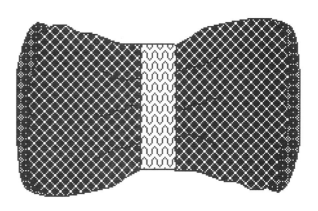

Illustration of Double Bow Pillow With Band

133

Boxed Pillow

DO NOT make a boxed needlepoint pillow UNLESS you have some experience in successfully making boxed pillows. Practice on muslin first. The inner pillow is made exatly as described on page 132. However, the dimensions are 2 inches larger than the needlepoint in both length and width.

Trim your needlepoint canvas and cut your backing to match. Your boxing band will be one and one half to two inches wide when finished. Be sure to leave seam allowances on either edge of the band. Cut your fabric strip two and one half to three inches wide, on the straight of the fabric. The length should be the perimeter of the finished pillow plus one inch extra for the seam allowance. If you are going to use cording or welting you will need twice as much and it should be attached to both front and back of your pillow, following the method described in the knife edged pillow above, sewing it to the right sides of the needlepoint and the backing.

Place your needlepoint on the boxing band (right sides together). The seam of the boxing band should fall at the center of the bottom side of the pillow. Stitch along on top of the welting stitches all the way around the piece. Clip the corners of the boxing band. Seam the two edges of the boxing band. Place the backing strip on the boxing band, right sides together. The right side of the fabric should be facing the right side of the needlepoint. Stitch all the way around except for an opening about six to eight inches long on the bottom side of the pillow. Turn right side out and stuff with the inner pillow you made earlier.Hand sew the opening closed with blind stitches. If you wish to use a zipper in a boxed pillow it is customary to insert it in the boxing band, on the bottom side of the pillow.

There are many more decorative techniques for making pillows. Look for an upholstery instruction book at your local library.

PREPARING NEEDLEPOINT FOR FRAMING

Materials Needed:

Stitched and Blocked Needlepoint
Stretcher Bars (Dimensions of the needlepoint or 1/4 inch plywood cut to size)
Muslin Fabric (Slightly larger than needlepoint)
White Seam Binding
Staples
White Glue
Thumb Tacks or Push Pins
10/2 Linen for Lacing

Clean and block your needlepoint in the usual manner. Trim canvas to within 2 and 1/2 inches of stitching. Stretch the muslin over the stretcher bars or plywood and staple in place. The muslin will protect your needlepoint from the acids in the wood. Use white glue to glue seam binding over staples all around perimeter of the wood. The seam binding will protect the needlepoint canvas from rust marks caused by the staples over the years. When glue has dried, place your needlepoint face down on a table and center the mounting board on the needlepoint.

Miter the corners but do not cut them.

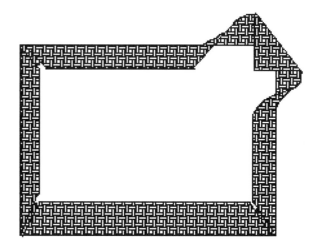

Mitering Diagram

You will find an additional illustration on mitering in the section on finishing a checkbook cover.

Tack your mitered corners with small stitches or use thumb tacks to hold in place temporarily.

You are now ready to lace your needlework. Thread a large-eyed needle with a long piece of linen cord. Make a knot at one end. Secure the knot to the canvas near any corner. Begin lacing back and forth as shown in accompanying picture. When you have completed lacing from side to side, repeat this process from top to bottom.

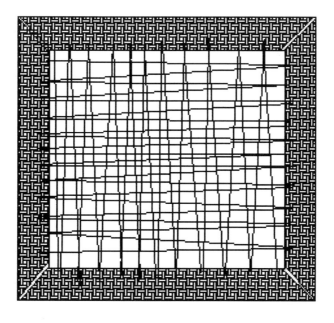

Lacing Diagram

135

Framing Your Needlepoint

If you know how to make picture frames, proceed to do so now. If not, do as we do and go to your local do-it-yourself framing store. You will find the people in charge very helpful and you will be amazed at how easy it is to make a professional looking frame.

Whether you go to a do-it-yourself shop or have a professional framer make your frame, we recommend that you block and mount the needlepoint yourself. Only then will you be sure that your needlepoint is mounted according to the above preservation method recommended by museum textile curators across the country.

Preservation Information

The following is up to the minute information supplied by restorers in the textile restoration department of the Cleveland Museum of Art. You may see contradictions in books published earlier. New information often disproves things once thought of as gospel.

Put glass over your needlework to protect it from the environment. However, do not use non-glare glass. Non glare glass is actually plastic containing minute black fibers which are not inert and could stain or even fuse to your work. Needlework should breathe so you must leave holes in the back of your frame.Use spacers to keep the glass from touching your work.

Do not use stain-retarding products on fine needlework. Such products have not been around long enough to have withstood the test of time. No one can predict how the chemicals in such products will react with the natural fibers or man-made dyes involved in your needlework.

In the preceding pages we have introduced you to the fundamentals of fiber art as expressed through the medium of needlepoint. Make no mistake - NEEDLEPOINT is an art. You the stitcher, are the artist. There are no limits to what your imagination and skill will allow you to create. Never be afraid to try something.The worst that can happen is a few hours of peaceful stitching with no finished product. Whatever you stitch will become part of the world that surrounds your friends and loved ones. In a way, that makes <u>you</u> immortal.

Kim and Iona

GLOSSARY OF ZWEIGART® CANVAS PRODUCTS

In this book many sizes and types of needlepoint canvas have been mentioned. Since very few shops carry every type of Zweigart® canvas in their inventory, a complete product list is being provided for your individual needs. You may write to the Zweigart® United States Sales Office: Joan Toggitt, Ltd., 2 Riverview Drive, Somerset, New Jersey 08873, for further information.

Item #	Canvas Name and Description			Mesh / Size
1281	**Apricot Toile**			
	Apricot	(270)	40" Width	18
	Apricot	(290)	40" Width	23
9406	**Congress Cloth**			
	White	(194)	50" Width	24
	Light Carmel	(294)	50" Width	24
	Ivory	(394)	50" Width	24
	Rose	(494)	50" Width	24
	Pale Blue	(594)	50" Width	24
	Grey	(794)	50" Width	24
	Black	(894)	50" Width	24
9500	**Double Mesh Canvas**			
	White	(026)	24" & 40" Width	6.5
	White	(030)	24" Width	7.5
	White	(038)	24" & 36" Width	10
	White	(048)	24" & 36" Width	12
	White	(056)	24" & 36" Width	14
	White	(060)	24" Width	16
	White	(070)	24" Width	18
	White	(080)	24" Width	20
9231	**Double Mesh Penelope Canvas**			
	White	(139)	36" Width	10
9604	Interlock Canvas			
	White	(040)	40" Width	10
	White	(048)	40" Width	12
	White	(052)	40" Width	13
	White	(056)	40" Width	14
	White	(070)	40" Width	18
9165	**Interlock Canvas**			
	White	(200)	40" Width	5
9699	**Interlock Canvas**			
	Ecru	(029)	48" Width	7
9605	**Interlock Canvas**			
	Brown	(040)	40" Width	10
	Brown	(048)	40" Width	12
	Brown	(056)	40" Width	14
9299	**Linen Canvas**			
	Off White	(052)	54" Width	13
	Off White	(068)	54" Width	17

Item #	Canvas Name and Description			Mesh / Size
9281	**Orange Line Mono Deluxe Canvas**			
	White	(040)	40" & 54" Width	10
	White	(046)	40" & 54" Width	12
	White	(052)	40" & 54" Width	13
	White	(056)	40" & 54" Width	14
	White	(060)	40" Width	16
	White	(070)	40" & 54" Width	18
1282	**Orange Line Mono Deluxe Canvas**			
	Brown	(040)	40" Width	10
	Brown	(046)	40" Width	12
	Brown	(052)	40" Width	13
	Brown	(056)	40" Width	14
	Brown	(070)	40" Width	18
9279	**Mono Standard Canvas**			
	White	(140)	36" Width	10
	White	(146)	36" Width	12
	White	(152)	36" Width	13
	White	(156)	36" Width	14
9010	**Royal Blue Line Petit Point Canvas**			
	Yellow	(002)	24" Width	17
0414	**Petit Point Canvas**			
	White	(088)	24" Width	22
	Yellow	(288)	24" Width	22
9213	**Double Mesh Quick Point Canvas**			
	White	(200)	40" Width	5
1231	**Double Mesh Quick Point Canvas**			
	Brown	(039)	36" Width	10
	Brown	(046)	36" Width	12
	Brown	(056)	36" Width	13
	Brown	(056)	36" Width	14
9124	**Rug Canvas**			
	Cream	(236)	40" Width	6
9106	**Rug Canvas**			
	Ecru	(132)	37" Width	3.3
	Ecru	(146)	37" & 43" Width	3.75
0698	**Rustic Canvas**			
	Natural	(048)	40" Width	12
1279	**Tan-Bargello Canvas**			
	Tan	(052)	27" & 36" Width	13
3938	**Toledo Soft Canvas**			
	Light Carmel	(250)	67" Width	30
0510	**Waste Canvas**			
	White	(026)	27" Width	6.5
	White	(034)	27" Width	8.5
	White	(038)	27" Width	10
	White	(044)	27" Width	11
	White	(048)	27" Width	12
	White	(052)	27" Width	13
	White	(056)	27" Width	14

GLOSSARY OF KREINIK SILK AND METALLIC THREADS

In this book many different kinds of silk and metallic threads have been mentioned. Since very few shops carry every type of Kreinik threads in their inventory, a product list is being provided for your individual needs. You may write to the Kreinik United States Marketing Office: Kreinik, 9199 Reisterstown Rd., Suite 209 B, Owings Mills, Maryland 21117, for further information.

SILK THREADS
Kreinik Thread Name and Description

Sole D'Alger	7 Ply Spun Silk - Moderate Luster - 450 Colors - Usage - All Needlework	3 or 4 Ply on 18 ct. Canvas 7 Ply on 13 Ct. Canvas 2 Ply Congress Cloth
Sole Gobelin	2 Ply Twisted Filament Silk - Usage - Needlepoint, Smocking, Cross Stitch	3 Ply on 18 Ct. Canvas
Sole Perlee	3 Ply Twisted Filament Silk - Usage - Needlepoint, Smocking, Cross Stitch	2 Ply on 18 Ct. Canvas
Sole Noppee	1 Ply Spun Silk - Usage - Needlepoint, Knitting, Crochet	1 Ply on 13 Ct. Canvas
Sole Platte	Untwisted Filament Silk - Flat Silk - Usage - Needlepoint	4 Ply on 18 Ct. Canvas
Ping Ling	6 Ply Filament Silk - Low Twist - 112 colors - Usage - Needlepoint	6 Ply on 18 Ct. Canvas

METAL THREADS
Kreinik Thread Name and Description

Blending Filament	Single Ply - Metallic Thread - May be blended with other threads or used alone - Available in three color types: Basic, Hi-Lustre, and Glow-In-The-Dark - Usage - Needlepoint or Cross Stitch
Cord	Tightly Wrapped Metallic Thread - Usage - An Accent Thread for Backstitching, Couching, Outlining or Adding a "Lacey" Effect when Cross Stitching - May be used for Machine Embroidery
Cable	3 Ply Twisted Metallic Cord - Usage - Outlining and Couching
Japan Threads	Non Tarnishing Gimp - Available in Gold, Silver and Copper - Thread Sizes - Super Fine #1, Fine #5, and Medium #7 - Usage - Fine Stitching, Outlining, Couching, and Laid Work
Ombre	8 Ply - Metallic Thread - 9 Variegated Colors - Gold - Silver - Pearl - May be used with other Threads or Used Alone - Usage - Machine Knitting, Needlepoint, Cross Stitch, or Crochet
Facets	Multi-dimensional Bead-like Yarn - Usage - Couching by Hand or Machine To Create Texture and Dimension

METALLIC BRAIDS AND RIBBONS
Kreinik Thread Name and Description

Braids	Flat - Strong - Soft - Lustrous - Do Not Ravel - Lays Flat When Stitched - Fine, Medium, and Heavy Weights - Over 100 Colors Available - Usage - Embroidery and Needlepoint
Ribbons	Flat - Strong - Soft - Lustrous - Do Not Ravel - Lays Flat When Stitch - 1/8" and 1/16" Widths - Over 100 Colors Available - Usage- Embroidery and Needlepoint

Index

A

Acids in Wood, 134
Acrylic Paint, 5
Algerian Eyelet Stitch, 84
Algerian Eyelet Variation Stitch, 85
Alpaca, 8
Alphabets, 97

B

Backing, 14, 16
Basketweave Directions, Right-handed Stitchers, 21
Basketweave Directions, Left-handed Stitchers, 25
Bargello Band for Double Bow Pillow, 112
Beads, 118
Bell Pull, 121
Berber Wool, 8
Bill Millan Belt, 123
Binding Stitch, **54**, 118 - 119, 130
Bird Cage, 12
Blending Filament, 8
Blocking, 6, 8, 113, 117, 122, 134
Running Colors, 117
T-pins, 117
Blocking Board, 117
Boxed Pillow, 134
Brick Stitch, 34
Buttonhole Bars Stitch, 87
Buttonhole Stitch, 86

C

Cable, 8
Canvas, 2-4
Congress Cloth, 3
Cutting, 4, 115
Distortion, 16
Double Thread, 2
Grain of Canvas, 3, 21, 25
Interlock, 3, 118
Joining, 115
Lacing Canvas, 135
Mono, 2, 118
Penelope, 2, 118
Petit Point Canvas, 3
Plastic Canvas, 118
Silk Gauze, 3
Waste, 3
Weave, 22
Zweigart®, 3, 100, 103, 107,112, 113
Cashmere Stitch, 43
Casing
Caution, 25
Chain Stitch, 18, **88**
Chainette, 8
Charming Glitters, 9, 118
Charts, Reading 11
Checkbook Cover, 123
Chemicals, 136

Cigarettes, 15
Cleaning, 15, 116
Liquid Detergents, 116
Cleveland Museum of Art, 136
Cloissonne® from Johnson Creative Arts, 8
Coasters, 125
Colors Running, 117
Compensating Stitches, 14, 16
Congress Cloth, 3
Contact™ Paper, 117
Continental Tent Stitch, 20
Horizontal Continental, 30
Vertical Continental, 31
Copy Center, 6
Cord, 8
Corduroy, 131
Cotton, 3, 7, 8, 10, 11
Cross Stitch, 8, **55**
Cross Stitches, 54
Binding Stitch, 54
Cross Stitch, 55
Double Leviathan Stitch, 62
Double Straight Cross Stitch, 56
Fern Stitch, 58
Four Color Interwoven Herringbone Stitch, 60
Herringbone Gone Wrong Stitch, 61
Herringbone Stitch, 59
Leviathan Stitch, 57
Long-Armed Cross Stitch, 63
Montenegrin Stitch, 64
Oblong Cross With Back Stitch, 65
Raised Cross Stitch, 66
Reverse Tvistom Knitting Variation Stitch, 67
Rhodes Stitch, 68
Rice Stitch, 69
Rice Stitch Rice Stitch, 69
Rice Stitch Variation, 70
Smyrna Cross Stitch, 71
Straight Cross Stitch or Upright Cross Stitch, 72
Tvistøm Stitch, 63
Upright Cross Stitch, 72
Van Dyke Stitch, 73
Waffle Stitch, 74
Cutting Canvas, 4
Cutting Yarns, 10

D

Darning Pattern Stitch, 36
Decorative Stitches, 84
Algerian Eyelet Stitch, 84
Algerian Eyelet Variation Stitch, 85
Buttonhole Bars Stitch, 87
Buttonhole Stitch, 86
Chain Stitch, 88
Diagonal Buttonhole Stitch, 89
Diagonal Leaf Stitch, 90
Diamond Eyelet Stitch, 91
French Knot, 92
Leaf Stitch, 93

Ribbed Wheels, 94
Ribbed Wheels Reverse Stitch, 94
Spider Web Stitch, 95
Star Stitch, 84
Turkey Work Stitch, 96
Decorative Techniques, 134
Designing Your Project, 113
Diagonal Buttonhole Stitch, 89
Diagonal Leaf Stitch, 90
Diagonal or Plaited Interlaced Stitch, 44
Diagonal Mosaic Stitch, 45
Diagonal Stitches, 43
Cashmere Stitch, 43
Diagonal Mosaic Stitch, 45
Diagonal or Plaited Interlaced Stitch, 44
Diagonal Stitch, 46
Gobelin Stitch Slanted, 47
Jacquard Stitch, 48
Knitting Stitch, 49
Milanese Stitch, 50
Mosaic Stitch, 51
Scotch Stitch, 52
Stem Stitch, 53
Diagonal Stitch, 46
Diagonal Striped Sampler, 103
Diagonal Tent Stitch, 19
Diamond Eyelet Stitch, 91
DMC, 6
DMC Medici Wool, 6
Do-it-Yourself, 136
Double Bow Pillow, 112, 133
Double Brick Stitch Variation, 35
Double Leviathan Stitch, 62
Double Straight Cross Stitch, 56
Downhill Stitch, 24
Dry-cleaning, 8

E
Embellishments, 9, 118
Embroidery Floss, 7
Embroidery Hoop, 5
Emery, 4
Environment, 136
Excess Dye, 117
Eyeglass Case, 125

F
Facets™, 8
Fern Stitch, 58
Fibers, 6
Cotton, 7, 8, 10, 11
Matte Cotton, 7
Silk Thread, 7
Finishing, 118 - 135
Bell Pull, 121, 122
Bill Millan Belt, 123
Binding Stitch, 54, 118 - 119, 130
Boxed Pillow, 134
Casing, 122

Checkbook Cover, 123
Coasters, 125
Corduroy, 131
Double Bow Pillow, 133
Eyeglass Case, 125
Fold-over Clutch Purse, 127
Framing, 136
Fringe, 130
Hand Finishing, 118
Inner Pillow, 132
Key Tag, 126
Knife-edged Pillow With Welting, 133
Knife-edged Pillow Without Welting, 132
Lacing Canvas, 135
Lining, 122, 124, 125, 127, 130
Machine Finishing, 136
Magnets, 126
Needlepoint Band, 133
Paper Back Book Cover, 127
Pillow, 132
Pillow Applique, 129
Pillow Tab, 129
Polyfil® Stuffing, 131
Preservation, 136
Professional, 118
Purse, 127
Rug, 130
Seam Binding, 135
Sewing, Stitching, 118
Scissors Case, 127
Stitching Line, 132
Tassels, 119, 130
Tissue Case, 128
Trigger CLoth, 131
Turkey Work, 130
Twisted Cord, 119
Velvet. 131
Wall Hanging, 130
Welting, 133
Florentine Stitches, 37 - 39
Floss, 7 - 8
Cotton Floss, 7
Rayon Floss, 8
Fold-over Clutch Purse, 127
Four Color Interwoven Herringbone Stitch, 60
Four Square Blocker™, 117
Frame, 5, 11
Mounting the Project on, 11
Roller Bar Frames, 12
Stretcher Bar Frame, 12
Framing, 118, 134 - 136
French Knot, 92
Fringe, 130

G
Garment Canvas, 3
Giant Rococco Stitch, 80
Glass over, Needlework, 136
Glitter, 9

Glitz, 9, 118
Glue, 134
Gobelin Droit Stitch, 40
Gobelin Stitch Slanted, 47
Grain of Canvas, 3, 21, 25
Grain of Yarn, 10

H
Half Cross Stitch, 20, **32**
Hand Finishing, 118
Herringbone Gone Wrong Stitch, 61
Herringbone Stitch, 59
Hoop, Embroidery, 5
Horizontal Intersection, 22 - 27
Horizontal Striped Sampler, Advanced, 107
Hungarian Ground Stitch, 41
Hyplar®, 113

I
Inner Pillow, 132
Intersection, 25, 26, 27

J
Jacquard Stitch, 48
Japan, 7
Japan Thread, 8
Joining Canvas, 115

K
Key Tag, 126
Kimonos, 7
Knife-edged Pillow With Welting, 133
Knife-edged Pillow Without Welting, 132
Knitting Stitch, 49
Knot, 135
Knotted Fringe, 130
Knotted Stitch Over Five Threads, 75
Knotting Yarn, 13
Knot Used in Lacing, 135
Waste Knot, 13
Kreinik Mfg. Co., Inc., 3, 7 -8
Kreinik Ombre®

L
Lacing Canvas, 135
Leaf Stitch, 93
Left-handed, 7
Left-handed Instructions, General, 15
Left-handed Basketweave Directions, 25
Leviathan Stitch, 57
Linen Canvas, 3
Linen Thread, 7, 11, 130
Lining, 122, 124, 125, 127, 130
Liquid Detergents, 116
Liquitex® Acrylic Paint, 5, 113
Long-Armed Cross Stitch, 63
Loop Method of Yarn Cutting, 10
Looped and Tied Sheaf Stitch, 77
Loop Stitch, 76

M
Machine Sewing, 118, 131
Magnets, 126
Marie Products, 117
Matte Cotton, 10, 11, 73
Medici Wool, 6, 10
Metal Thread, 8
Bullion, 8
Japan Thread, 8
Purl, 8
Metallic Thread, 8
Blending Filament, 8
Cable, 8
Chainette, 8
Cloissonne from Johnson Creative Art, 8
Cord, 8
Facets, 8
Kreinik Ombre®
Ribbon, 8
Milanese Stitch, 50
Mistakes, 14
Mitered Corners, 123, 135
Monogram Alphabet, 98
Montenegrin Stitch, 8, **64**
Mounting the Project on a Frame, 11
Mosaic Stitch, 51
Muslin, 131, 134

N
Needle Threader, 4
Needles, 4
Needlepoint Canvas, 2 - 4
Needlepoint Band, 133
Nepo® Marking Pen, 5
Newspapers, 12, 15, 17
Newsprint, 6
Notions and Accessories, 4
Nylons, 7

O
Oblong Cross With Back Stitch, 65
Outlining, 8
Oversized Projects, 114

P
Paint with Yarn, 6
Pansy Centered Sampler...100
Paper Needle Threader, 4 - 5
Paper, 6
Graph paper, 6
Newsprint, 6
Tracing Paper, 6
Paperback Book Cover, 127
Patent Leather, 8
Penelope Canvas, 2, 20
Perle Cotton, 10
Persian Yarn, 7, 10
Petit Point, 3
Pets, 15

Pillow, 132
Boxed Pillow, 134
Knife-edged Pillow With Welting, 133
Knife-edged Pillow Without Welting, 132
Pillow Applique, 129
Pillow Tab, 129
Pin Cushion, 4
Ping Ling, 7
Plaited Interlaced Stitch, 44
Plan Project, 114
Ply, 14
Polyester Garment Canvas, 3
Polyfil® Stuffing, 131
Polished Silk, 7
Pre-finished Pillow, 129
Preservation, 136
Professional, 118
Projects, 99 -113, 114, 121 - 130
Bargello Band for Double Bow Pillow, 112
Bell Pull, 121
Bill Millan Belt, 123
Boxed Pillow, 134
Checkbook Cover, 123
Coasters, 125
Designing Your Project, 113
Diagonal Striped Sampler, 103
Eyeglass Case, 125
Horizontal Striped Sampler, Advanced, 107
Fold-over Clutch Purse, 127
Joining Canvas, 115
Key Tag, 126
Knife-edged Pillow With Welting, 133
Knife-edged Pillow Without Welting, 132
Large Rug in Sections, 115
Lining, 122, 124, 126
Magnets, 126
Needlepoint Band, 133
Pansy Centered Sampler, 100
Pillow Applique, 129
Pillow Tab, 129
Planning, 114
Paper Back Book Cover, 127
Pillow Applique, 129
Pillow Tab, 129
Purse, 127
Rug, 115, 130
Scissors Case, 127
Tissue Case, 128
Wall Hanging, 130
Preservation, 136
Purse, 127

R
Raised Cross Stitch, 66
Rayon, 7, 8, 11
Cord, 8
Floss, 8
Ribbon, 8
Synthetic Silk, 8

Renaissance Rococco Stitch, 78
Repair of cut canvas, 4, 14
Reverse Tvistom Knitting Variation Stitch, 67
Rhinestones, Sew-on, 9
Rhodes Stitch, 68
Ribbed Wheels, 94
Ribbed Wheels Reverse Stitch, 94
Ribbon, 8
Ribbon Roses, 118
Rice Stitch, 69
Rice Stitch Variation, 70
Right-handed Basketweave Directions, 21
Rococco Stitch, 79
Roller Bar Frames, 12
Rug, 130
Running Colors, 117

S
Sampler, 16
Sampler Projects, 99
Bargello Band for Double Bow Pillow, 112
Diagonal Striped Sampler, 103
Horizontal Striped Sampler, Advanced, 107
Pansy Centered Sampler, 100
Sanford Nepo® Marking Pen, 5
Scissors, 4, 14
Dress-making scissors, 4
Embroidery scissors, 4
Scissors Case, 127
Scoop Stitching, 15
Scotch Stitch, 8, **52**
Seam Binding, 135
Seam Ripper, 4
Selvage, 17, 122
Sewing, 118
Sew-on Rhinestones, 9
Sheaf Stitch, 81
Silk, 3, 7, 11
Ping Ling, 7
Polished Silk, 7
Silk Thread, 7
Silk Gauze Canvas, 3
Silkworm Moth, 7
Soie d'Alger, 7
Soie Gobelins, 7
Soie Noppee, 7
Soie Perlee, 7
Soie Platte, 7
Treated Silk, 7
Waterlilies™, 8
Smoking, 15, 17
Smyrna Cross Stitch, 71
Snacks, 15
Soie d'Alger, 7
Soie Gobelins, 7
Soie Noppee, 7
Soie Perlee, 7
Soie Platte, 7
Spider Web Stitch, 95

Spritz, 117
Stain Retardent Materials, 136
Staples, 12
Star Stitch, 84
Stem Stitch, 53
Stepped Sheaf Ground Stitch, 82
Stitch Clean™, 116
Stitches, 16
Algerian Eyelet Stitch, 84
Algerian Eyelet Variation Stitch, 85
Basketweave Directions, Right-handed, 21
Basketweave Directions, Left-handed, 25
Binding Stitch, 54
Brick Stitch, 34
Buttonhole Bars Stitch, 87
Buttonhole Stitch, 86
Cashmere Stitch, 43
Chain Stitch, 88
Continental Tent Stitch, 20
Cross Stitch, 55
Darning Pattern Stitch, 36
Diagonal Buttonhole Stitch, 89
Diagonal Leaf Stitch, 90
Diagonal Mosaic Stitch, 45
Diagonal or Plaited Interlaced Stitch, 44
Diagonal Stitch, 46
Diagonal Stitches, 43
Diagonal Tent Stitch, 19
Diamond Eyelet Stitch, 91
Double Brick Stitch Variation, 35
Double Leviathan Stitch, 62
Double Straight Cross Stitch, 56
Fern Stitch, 58
Four Color Interwoven Herringbone Stitch, 60
Florentine Stitches, 37 - 39
French Knot, 92
Giant Rococco Stitch, 80
Gobelin Droit Stitch, 40
Gobelin Stitch Slanted, 47
Herringbone Gone Wrong Stitch, 61
Herringbone Stitch, 59
Hungarian Ground Stitch, 41
Jacquard Stitch, 48
Knitting Stitch, 49
Knotted Stitch Over Five Threads, 75
Leaf Stitch, 93
Leviathan Stitch, 57
Long-Armed Cross Stitch, 63
Loop Stitch, 76
Looped and Tied Sheaf Stitch, 77
Milanese Stitch, 50
*Montenegrin Stitch, 8, **64***
Mosaic Stitch, 51
Oblong Cross With Back Stitch, 65
Raised Cross Stitch, 66
Renaissance Rococco Stitch, 78
Reverse Tvistom Knitting Variation Stitch, 67
Ribbed Wheels, 94
Ribbed Wheels Reverse Stitch, 94

Rhodes Stitch, 68
Rice Stitch, 69
Rice Stitch Variation, 70
Rococco Stitch, 79
*Scotch Stitch, 8, **52***
Sheaf Stitch, 81
Shell Stitch, 77
Smyrna Cross Stitch, 71
Spider Web Stitch, 95
Stem Stitch, 53
Stepped Sheaf Ground Stitch, 82
Straight Stitches, 33
Straight Cross Stitch or Upright Cross Stitch, 72
Tent Stitches, 17
Tied Stitches, 75
Tvistøm Stitch, 63
*Turkey Work Stitch, **96**, 130*
Upright Cross Stitch, 72
Van Dyke Stitch, 73
Victorian Step Stitch, 42
*Waffle Stitch, 8, **74***
Web Stitch. 83
Stitching, 118, 132
Stitching Line, 132
Straight Cross Stitch or Upright Cross Stitch, 72
Straight Stitches, 33
Brick Stitch, 34
Darning Pattern Stitch, 36
Double Brick Stitch Variation, 35
Florentine Stitches, 37 - 39
Gobelin Droit Stitch, 40
Hungarian Ground Stitch, 41
Victorian Step Stitch, 42
Stretcher Bar Frame, 12, 134
Stuffing, 131
Synthetic Silk, 8

T
Tape, 14
Tapestry Wool, 6
Tassels, 119, 132
Tension, 14
Tent Stitches, 17
Continental Tent Stitch, 20
Diagonal Tent Stitch, 19
Textile Restoration Department, 136
T-pins, 117
Tied Stitches, 75
Giant Rococco Stitch, 80
Knotted Stitch Over Five Threads, 75
Loop Stitch, 76
Looped and Tied Sheaf Stitch, 77
Renaissance Rococco Stitch, 78
Rococco Stitch, 79
Sheaf Stitch, 81
Shell Stitch, 77
Stepped Sheaf Ground Stitch, 82
Web Stitch. 83
Threader, Needle, 4

Threading the Needle, 4, 13
Threads, 6 - 8
Crewel Wool, 6
Linen Thread, 7
Matte Cotton, 7
Medici Wool, 6, 10
Persian Wool, 6, 10,
Tapestry Wool, 6
Tied Stitches, 75
Tissue Case, 128
Tomato Pin Cushion, 4
Tracing Paper, 6
Treated Silk, 7
Trigger Cloth, 131
Trimming Canvas, 131
Trims, 119
Turkey Work Stitch, **96**, 130
Turning Stitch, 23, 27
Tvistøm Stitch, 63
Twisted Cord, 119
Twisted Cotton, 8

U
Ultra Suede®, 8
UnStitch Gremlin, 116
Uphill Stitch, 23
Upholstery Instruction Book, 134
Upright Cross Stitch, 72

V
Van Dyke Stitch, 73
Veloura, 8
Velvet, 131
Vertical Intersection, 22 - 27
Victorian Step Stitch, 42

W
Waffle Stitch, 8, **74**
Wall Hanging, 130
Warp Thread, 4, 14
Warped Canvas, 122
Waste Knot, 13
Watercolors™, 8
Waterlilies™, 8
Waterproof Pen, 5, 12
Web Stitch. 83
Welting, 133
Weft Thread, 4, 14
Wood Acids, 134
Wool, 7, 8, 9
Berber Wool, 8
DMC Medici Wool, 6
Paterna™, 100, 103, 107, 112
Persian Wool, 6
Wool, 6
Working Conditions, 15

Y
Yarn, Cutting, 10
Yarn Thickness, 14

Z
Zweigart®, 3, 100, 103, 107,112, 113

Bibliography

Berman, Jennifer and Lazarus, Carole, The Glorafilia Needlepoint Collection, Devon UK, 1989. David and Charles Publishers plc., Newton Abbot, Devon UK

Christensen, Jo Ippolito, The Needlepoint Book, New Jersey, 1976, Prentice-Hall, Inc. Englewood Cliffs, New Jersey

Felcher, Cecelia The Needlepoint Workbook of Traditional Designs, New York 1973, Hawthorn Books, Inc. 260 Madison Ave, New York, N.Y. 10016

Field, Peggy and Linsley, June, Canvas Embroidery, London 1990, Merehurst Limited, Ferry House, 51-57 Lacy Road, Putney, London SW15 1PR

Geddes, Elisabeth and McNeill, Moyra, Blackwork Embroidery, London, England 1965 Mills and Boon, Ltd., 17-19 Foley St., London, W1A, 1DR, England

Gantt, Joan Durstine, Lexington Lace, Dallas, Texas 1975, Heritage Designs, 3512 Lexington Ave., Dallas, Texas 75205

Ireys, Katherine, The Encyclopedia of Canvas Embroidery Stitch Patterns, New York, 1968, Thomas Y. Crowell Co., 201 Park Ave.. South, New York, N. Y. 10003

Kennett, Frances and Scarlett, Belinda, Country House Needlepoint, London, England, 1988, Conran Octopus, Ltd., 37 Shelton St., London WC2H 9HN

Lantz, Shirlee and Lane, Maggie, A Pageant of Pattern for Needlepoint Canvases, New York, 1973, Atheneum Press, New York, New York.

Rhodes, Mary, Needlepoint, the Art of Canvas Embroidery, London, England, 1974, Octopus Books Ltd., 59 Grosvenor St,. London W1

Rome, Carol Cheney and Devlin, Georgia French, A New Look at Needlepoint, New York, 1972, Crown Publishers, Inc., 419 Park Ave. South, New York, N.Y. 10016

Russell, Beth, Victorian Needlepoint, London, England 1989, Anaya Publishers, Ltd., 49 Neal St., London WC2H 9P, second reprint February 1991

notes

notes

notes